Great Taste ~ Low Fat

CHICKEN

TIME
LIFE
BOOKS

ALEXANDRIA, VIRGINIA

TABLE OF CONTENTS

Introduction *4*

Secrets of Low-Fat Cooking *6*

Mediterranean

Chicken Salad

∿

page 23

Soups & Salads

Caribbean Chicken Salad *13*

Louisiana-Style Chicken Gumbo *15*

Lemon-Dill Chicken and Rice Soup *16*

Taco Salad with Tomato-Avocado Salsa *19*

Hearty Chicken and Corn Chowder *21*

Mediterranean Chicken Salad *23*

Chicken and White Bean Salad *24*

Oriental Chicken Soup *25*

Broiled Chicken and Orange Salad *27*

Creamy Chicken Soup with Vegetables *28*

Chicken and Potato Salad *31*

Chinese Chicken Salad with Peanuts *33*

Chicken and Winter Vegetable Soup *34*

Chicken Tabbouleh Salad *37*

Mom's Chicken Noodle Soup *39*

New Deli Chicken Salad *41*

Chicken Cobb Salad *42*

Braises & Stews

Savory Chicken, Carrot, and Potato Stew *45*

Spiced Chicken Couscous *47*

Chicken and Apples Normandy *48*

Oven-Braised Rosemary Chicken with Vegetables *50*

Chicken in Red Wine Sauce *51*

Chicken with Winter Squash and Artichokes *53*

Chunky Chicken and Corn Chili *55*

Chicken Jambalaya *56*

Chicken in Green Sauce *57*

Chicken Goulash with Egg Noodles *58*

Chicken with Tomatoes and Chick-Peas *61*

Parslied Chicken and Dumplings *63*

Port-Braised Chicken with Carrots and Parsnips *65*

Chicken Picante *66*

Chicken Fricassee with Leeks and Peas *69*

Arroz con Pollo *70*

Baked & Roasted

Chili-"Fried" Chicken with Rice Pilaf *73*

Herbed Chicken with Orzo and Spinach *74*

Chicken Pot Pie *77*

Roast Chicken with Pecan-Rice Dressing *79*

Chicken Burgers with Sweet Potato Chips *81*

Glazed Honey-Mustard Chicken *82*

Chicken Parmesan with Herbed Tomatoes *83*

Lemon Chicken with
Roast Potatoes and Garlic

〜

page 91

Buffalo Chicken Strips *84*

Baked Chicken in Parchment *86*

Asian Chicken Roll-Ups *87*

Chicken and Sweet Potatoes with Rosemary *89*

Lemon Chicken with Roast Potatoes and Garlic *91*

Spinach-and-Cheese-Stuffed Chicken *93*

Oven-Barbecued Chicken Breasts *94*

Chicken, Vegetables, and Corn Bread Casserole *95*

Baked Chicken with Citrus Sauce *97*

Crispy Chicken with Corn Chowchow *98*

Mustard-Crumb Chicken Breasts *101*

Easy Chicken, Red Beans, and Rice *102*

Sautés & Stir-Fries

Chicken Stir-Fry with Broccoli, Garlic, and Basil *105*

Sweet and Sour Chicken *106*

Fajita-Style Fettuccine *107*

Chicken, Corn, and Zucchini Sauté *108*

East-West Chicken Stir-Fry *111*

Chicken and Potatoes with Penne *112*

Fettuccine with Chicken and Tangy Onion Sauce *113*

Chicken Scallopini with Chunky Tomato Sauce *115*

Chicken with Spaghetti and Summer Squash *116*

Stir-Fried Chicken and Asparagus with Linguine *119*

Curried Chicken Breasts with Coconut Rice *120*

Spanish-Style Chicken *121*

Chicken-Fried Pasta *123*

Stir-Fried Chicken with Peppers and Snow Peas *125*

Chicken Cacciatore *126*

Broiled & Grilled

Chicken Dijonnaise *129*

Onion-Smothered Chicken *130*

Salsa-Marinated Chicken *133*

Chicken Breasts with Pineapple-Pepper Relish *134*

Barbecued Chicken with Beans *135*

Chicken and Vegetable Kabobs *137*

Hot and Tangy Barbecued Chicken with Noodles *139*

Chicken with Chili Corn Sauce *140*

Broiled Chicken with Apricot-Lemon Sauce *143*

Herbed Chicken Breasts with Lentils *144*

Spicy Jamaican-Style Chicken Thighs *145*

Chicken with Plum Tomato Salsa *147*

Lemon Chicken Kabobs *148*

Maple-Broiled Chicken *151*

Chicken Teriyaki *153*

〜

Glossary *154*

Index *157*

Credits *159*

Metric Conversion Charts *160*

INTRODUCTION

Our mission at Great Taste-Low Fat is to take the work and worry out of everyday low-fat cooking; to provide delicious, fresh, and filling recipes for family and friends; to use quick, streamlined methods and available ingredients; and, within every recipe, to keep the percentage of calories from fat under 30 percent.

Chicken—once a symbol of universal prosperity (remember "A chicken in every pot"?)—deserves all praise as a food that is nutritionally close to perfect. Low in fat yet satisfying, chicken pleases the palate by absorbing the bold or delicate flavors surrounding it while it cooks. It cooks quickly, and contains just enough fat and sugar to brown beautifully and contribute depth and richness to a low-fat sauce. And, perhaps most important, chicken is delicious—at least the way we cook it.

COMMON-SENSE TECHNIQUES

The challenge of creating so many delicious, low-fat, satisfying, and easy chicken recipes is a formidable one, especially since we use only ingredients that are readily available nationwide. Our talented and experienced chefs rose to the task by drawing on both their culinary expertise and old-fashioned common sense to streamline the recipes and make use of every bit of flavor. To them, the marriage of low-fat and quick cooking is a natural one, because the shorter cooking time keeps the chicken moist (slow-cooking methods require the insulating properties of fat to prevent the meat from drying out). Our chefs were also delighted to be able to provide large portions and use ingredients that go beyond traditional low-fat fare, such as Canadian bacon, egg noodles, and light sour cream—we use just enough to add flavor, but not a lot of fat.

The techniques we use are simple. Chopping the ingredients into small pieces, for example, exposes more surface area, allowing faster cooking and greater absorption of flavor. Adding modest amounts of oil to a skillet before sautéing moistens the ingredients and releases the flavors to the entire dish. Removing the skin *after* roasting chicken results in juicier meat (the skin keeps the moisture in and the fat doesn't transfer to the meat during cooking). And using thighs and drumsticks occasionally—rather than the usual breast meat—retains moisture and adds flavor, especially to hearty dishes. Through proper use of low-fat dairy products and time-honored thickeners we show you how to produce mouth-watering, creamy sauces. And by using intensely flavored ingredients you can easily compensate for the loss of flavor that accompanies the reduction of fat.

VARIETY OF ENTRÉES

This book is divided into five chapters, by type of entrée. The first, Soups and Salads, gives a tempting variety of salads, from a homey chicken and potato salad to a Caribbean-inspired treat with mango, as well as hearty soups for all seasons. In Braises and Stews you'll find rich, robust recipes unlike anything you've seen in other low-fat cookbooks: a goulash with egg noodles and sour cream; a stew with light, fluffy dumplings (we show you how to make them with an illustrated tip); and an amazingly quick and delicious chicken chili. Baked and Roasted gives easy one-dish casseroles that have exciting twists like a corn bread "crust," and even a cream-cheese stuffing for roasted chicken breasts. Sautés and Stir-fries provides a chunky scallopini, thick, puréed sauces made from such unusual ingredients as roasted red peppers and even bananas, and the fabulous Chicken-Fried Pasta, which must be tasted to be believed. Finally, Broiled and Grilled elevates these cooking methods to new, filling, flavorful heights with delicious and innovative sauces.

Our "Secrets of Low-Fat Cooking" section will set the stage for low-fat satisfaction with flavor enhancers to stock up on, techniques for handling chicken, and some illustrations of our most commonly used cooking methods. And, of course, every recipe will help you along with informative headnotes and, if additional guidance is useful, an illustrated tip.

Please enjoy the fabulous recipes and full color photos in this exciting cookbook, because the more you use it, the closer you'll come to knowing that you *can* eat right every night.

CONTRIBUTING EDITORS

Sandra Rose Gluck, a New York City chef, has years of experience creating delicious low-fat recipes that are quick to prepare. Her secret for satisfying results is to always aim for great taste and variety. By combining readily available, fresh ingredients with simple cooking techniques, Sandra has created the perfect recipes for today's busy lifestyles.

Grace Young has been the director of a major test kitchen specializing in low-fat and health-related cookbooks for over 12 years. Grace oversees the development, taste testing, and nutritional analysis of every recipe in Great Taste-Low Fat. Her goal is simple: take the work and worry out of low-fat cooking so that you can enjoy delicious, healthy meals every day.

Kate Slate has been a food editor for almost 20 years, and has published thousands of recipes in cookbooks and magazines. As the Editorial Director of Great Taste-Low Fat, Kate combined simple, easy to follow directions with practical low-fat cooking tips. The result is guaranteed to make your low-fat cooking as rewarding and fun as it is foolproof.

NUTRITION

Every recipe in *Great Taste-Low Fat* provides per-serving values for the nutrients listed in the chart at right. The daily intakes listed in the chart are based on those recommended by the USDA and presume a nonsedentary lifestyle. The nutritional emphasis in this book is not only on controlling calories, but on reducing total fat grams. Research has shown that dietary fat metabolizes more easily into body fat than do carbohydrates and protein. In order to control the amount of fat in a given recipe and in your diet in general, no more than 30 percent of the calories should come from fat.

Nutrient	Women	Men
Fat	<65 g	<80 g
Calories	2000	2500
Saturated fat	<20 g	<25 g
Carbohydrate	300 g	375 g
Protein	50 g	65 g
Cholesterol	<300 mg	<300 mg
Sodium	<2400 mg	<2400 mg

These recommended daily intakes are averages used by the Food and Drug Administration and are consistent with the labelling on all food products. Although the values for cholesterol and sodium are the same for all adults, the other intake values vary depending on gender, ideal weight, and activity level. Check with a physician or nutritionist for your own daily intake values.

SECRETS OF LOW-FAT COOKING

CHICKEN

The healthful qualities of chicken lend themselves beautifully to the various cooking methods in this cookbook. In "Secrets of Low-Fat Cooking," we provide you with all the information you'll need about basic cooking equipment, essential pantry items, buying and handling chicken, and commonly used cooking techniques to ensure your success in making our delicious, satisfying low-fat recipes.

THE LOW-FAT KITCHEN

To get started, you need only a few pieces of cooking equipment and a handful of pantry staples:

• Equipment: A nonstick skillet, which eliminates or minimizes the need for fat in cooking, is essential to making low-fat dishes. A nonstick Dutch oven is also convenient to have for cooking in quantity. Choose pans that are sturdy but not too heavy to lift and maneuver comfortably. Be sure lids are snug fitting and handles securely attached. Nonstick skillets with ridges let you cook meats over high heat while the fat drains away from the food. A rack for roasting or broiling accomplishes the same result.

• Reduced-Fat Dairy Products: A whole range of new nonfat, low-fat, and reduced-fat dairy products make possible sensible versions of formerly fatty dishes, such as goulash. Many of the sauces,

soups, and stews in this book use reduced-fat dairy products to create a satisfying creamy richness, or pleasing "mouth feel." For most cooking purposes, a reduced-fat or "light" dairy product is the best choice. Nonfat dairy products should be used judiciously, since flavor and texture may be lacking, and cooking may cause them to separate and possibly curdle. An exception is nonfat yogurt, which can usually be substituted for regular yogurt.

For creamier stews and sauces, rely on nonfat yogurt (mixed with a little flour to stabilize it), stirred into the stew toward the end of cooking. Reduced-fat sour cream may be stirred into a cooked dish, but only at the end of cooking, off the heat. Evaporated skimmed milk lends noticeable body to soups, stews, and sauces. Buttermilk, a low-fat dairy product made by adding lactic acid cultures to skim milk, gives tang to salad dressings and dumplings. It can also be used as a marinade for oven-fried chicken before the dry coating is added. Reduced-fat cheeses are good in such dishes as dips and under-the-skin poultry stuffings.

• Other Thickeners: Besides the dairy products that act as thickeners, there are several basic pantry items that can be used to thicken sauces. Flour makes an opaque sauce, while cornstarch creates a clear one, and requires less cooking than flour. Tomato paste adds thickness, sweetness, and color.

FLAVOR ENHANCERS

In low-fat cooking, highly flavored ingredients are used to replace the flavor-carrying qualities of fat. Essential flavorings used in this book include:

• Herbs and spices, which add flavor and fragrance to any dish. Use fresh herbs when available.

• Acidic ingredients, such as citrus juices and vinegars, which give a pleasantly complex sharpness.

• Citrus zest (see box at right).

• Sweet ingredients. Dried fruits (including sun-dried tomatoes), honey, and maple syrup are used to soften the acidity in a tart dish.

• Salty ingredients. Soy sauce, Parmesan cheese, and olives are used to lift the flavors in a recipe. They are always used in moderation.

• Flavorful oils. Using olive oil or sesame oil for cooking adds a subtle intensity.

• Nuts, especially toasted, used in small amounts for an appealing crunch and flavor.

• Wines and spirits for a deep, earthy bite.

• Onion-flavored ingredients, such as garlic, shallots, and scallions. Cooking tames their pungency.

• Hot peppers and their derivatives, to give mild dishes a welcome bit of fire.

Basil

Rosemary

Garlic

Scallions

Lime

Lemon

Orange

Salt and
Pepper

Cider Vinegar

Olive Oil

Red Wine Vinegar

Red Wine

Oriental
Sesame Oil

Parmesan
Cheese

Ginger

Red Pepper
Flakes

Dried
Tarragon

Honey

Soy Sauce

Chili Peppers

Peanuts

Currants

Sun-Dried
Tomatoes

Golden Raisins

Olives

Dried Apricots

Zesting

The colored outer part of citrus peel, called
zest, is full of intensely flavored oils that can
add a fresh zing to any dish. To remove
zest, while avoiding the bitter white pith
underneath, use a fine-holed grater, a citrus
zester for long thin curls (pictured above),
or a vegetable peeler for wider strips that
can then be thinly slivered or chopped.

BUYING CHICKEN SENSIBLY

Not all parts of a chicken are created equal when it comes to fat. Three and one-half ounces of cooked meat from chicken wings, with skin, have a whopping 20 grams of fat. An equivalent portion of skinless breast meat is a much wiser choice at only four grams of fat. For skinless dark meat, which is used in many of our recipes for both its bolder flavor and its tendency to retain moisture during cooking, the tally is 10 grams of fat. Whether you choose white or dark meat, remember that removing the skin either before or after cooking can reduce the total fat by up to 50 percent.

When buying whole chickens, look for birds with plump, rounded breasts. Press against the tip of the breastbone; if it's pliable, the chicken is young and the meat will be tender. Chicken parts should also be plump. Whether a chicken is yellow or white depends on the breed and has no bearing on quality or nutritional value. For frozen chicken, choose the package from the bottom of the case, where it's coldest. Frozen chicken should be rock hard, without frozen liquid in the package, a sign that the chicken has thawed and been refrozen.

HANDLING CHICKEN

Refrigerate raw chicken in its original wrapping for up to two days or freeze, overwrapped with plastic wrap or foil, for up to two months. Thaw frozen chicken overnight in the refrigerator, never at room temperature. To prevent any bacteria present in raw chicken from spreading to other foods, do not let the chicken come in contact with foods, and wash work surfaces, utensils, and hands with hot, soapy water after handling chicken. When cutting chicken, it's best to use a plastic board because it can be cleaned more thoroughly than a wooden one. If you must use a wooden board, keep it exclusively for preparing raw meats, and use a separate board for breads and vegetables. The USDA recommends cooking boneless chicken to an internal temperature of 160°, bone-in parts to 170°, and whole birds to 180°, or until the juices run clear and the flesh is white rather than pink.

Skinning Legs and Breasts

To skin a whole chicken leg, lightly cut skin around the joint between drumstick and thigh with a paring knife. Holding end of thigh, gently loosen skin around cut at joint, slip fingers under skin, and gently pull off. Repeat procedure with drumstick portion.

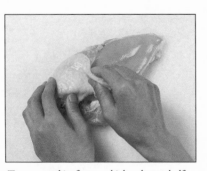

To remove skin from a chicken breast half on the bone, gently loosen skin at narrow end of breast. Holding opposite end with one hand, slip your fingers under the loosened skin and gently pull off, turning the breast as you work.

Splitting Whole Legs

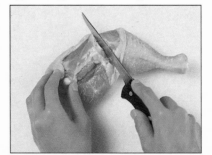

Place the chicken leg, skin-side down, on a clean cutting board, and slightly stretch the drumstick and thigh apart to find the ball joint. With a sharp boning knife, cleanly cut through the joint, using a firm, downward motion.

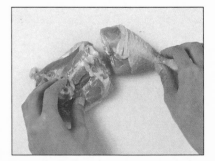

Grabbing the leg at opposite ends, pull apart the thigh and drumstick. If you need only drumsticks or thighs for a recipe, purchasing whole chicken legs and splitting them yourself will save you money. Wrap and freeze whichever part you don't need.

To infuse subtle flavor into chicken without introducing extra fat, place a stuffing under the skin before roasting or baking. It's fine to leave the skin on the chicken, because no significant amount of fat is transferred from the skin to the meat during cooking. In addition, the skin prevents the chicken from drying out. Just be sure to remove the poultry skin before eating. This stuffing technique works equally well with whole chickens or any chicken part with skin.

Placing Stuffing Under Skin

For a bone-in chicken breast half, first loosen edges of skin with your fingers. Gently push fingers between skin and meat, without tearing skin, to form a pocket. Place the stuffing under skin, then ease skin back to its original position.

When working with a whole chicken, loosen edges of skin along breasts at back end of bird. Gently separate skin from meat on both sides of breast, forming a pocket. Push stuffing into the pocket, spreading it evenly over meat. Then ease skin back to cover stuffing.

Chicken thigh meat is becoming increasingly popular, especially for stews and braises, since it remains flavorfully moist during long cooking. Its richness works in sautés and stir-fries, too. Boning out the thighs lets you cut the meat into any shape—cubes, dice, julienne—and eliminates the messiness of dealing with the bones while eating. While boneless thighs are available in supermarkets, boning them yourself is less expensive and yields the extra bonus of bones for stock.

Boning Thighs

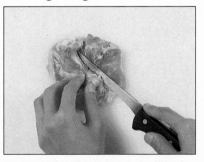

To begin, place the chicken thigh, skin-side down, on a clean cutting board. Using a long thin boning knife, score meat down the center, without cutting all the way through the meat. Press the thigh flat to open, as for a book, with bone in the center.

Scrape knife around ends of bone, loosening meat. Run knife down length of bone with little cuts, keeping knife as close to the bone as possible and working along all sides to free the meat. Cut around remaining end and lift out bone.

Homemade Chicken Broth

Many of our recipes call for canned broth, which is convenient and tasty. If you have time, though, make a batch of this homemade broth and freeze it in small containers—it will always add flavor and body to a recipe, and contains much less sodium than even reduced-sodium canned broth. Leave the skin on the chicken legs for flavor; any fat in the broth will be skimmed off at the end. This makes about 7 cups broth; you may refrigerate for up to 3 days or freeze for up to 6 months.

5 pounds whole chicken legs	1 carrot, thinly sliced
4 cloves garlic	1 tomato, coarsely chopped
1 large unpeeled onion, cut in half	½ teaspoon dried rosemary
1 leek, white and light green parts, thinly sliced	½ teaspoon dried thyme
1 rib celery, thinly sliced	6 sprigs parsley
	2 bay leaves

1. Preheat the oven to 400°. On a large baking sheet, spread the chicken and roast for 35 minutes, or until browned and crisp.

2. With tongs or a slotted spoon, transfer the chicken to a large stockpot. Pour off all fat from the baking sheet. Pour ½ cup water onto the baking sheet, scrape up any browned bits, and add to the stockpot. Pour in enough cold water to cover the chicken. Bring to a boil over high heat, skimming off any surface foam.

3. Add the garlic, onion, leek, celery, carrot, tomato, rosemary, thyme, parsley, and bay leaves. Return to a boil over high heat, skimming off any surface foam. Reduce to a simmer and cook, partially covered, until the broth is rich and flavorful, about 2 hours.

4. Strain the broth through a colander lined with cheesecloth and discard the solids. Cool slightly. Refrigerate the broth for at least 8 hours or overnight. Before using, remove the fat that has solidified on the surface.

LOW-FAT COOKING TECHNIQUES

Our cooking techniques not only reduce fat in the recipes, but offer ways to intensify the flavor to compensate for the lowered fat in the dish. For example, caramelizing means to cook meats and vegetables, especially onions, until the natural sugars have deeply browned, creating a rich base for pan-cooked preparations, such as our Sweet and Sour Chicken (page 106). Reducing or boiling off liquid in a mixture causes the flavors to become concentrated and mingle together deliciously in the pan. In another easy method, browning chicken after it is dredged in flour heightens the flavor of the finished stew or braise.

Caramelizing

To caramelize, cook the ingredients in a nonstick skillet, with little or no fat, over low to medium-low heat, until browned and meltingly tender. Stir occasionally to prevent sticking. Caramelizing will take a minimum of eight minutes or so.

Reducing

Reducing or cooking off liquid is a simple method for concentrating flavors. Add desired liquid to the browned ingredients in the nonstick skillet, bring to a boil over medium to medium-high heat, and continue to cook off the liquid until reduced by half or totally reduced, according to the recipe. Stir the mixture occasionally with a plastic spatula or wooden spoon. Never use a metal spatula, which could scratch the specially treated nonstick surface of the pan.

Dredging, an old-fashioned culinary technique, is still very much at home in contemporary low-fat cooking. Coating thin pieces of meat, such as skinless, boneless chicken breasts or cutlets, with a small amount of seasoned flour (or, for a mildly crunchy coating, cornmeal or bread crumbs) produces a tasty coating, lending textural contrast as well as sealing in flavor and moisture. A quick pre-browning of the coated food intensifies the flavor of the coating, adding to the complexity of the finished dish. If creating a pan sauce is part of the recipe, the browned bits of flour from the coating left in the bottom of the skillet will help thicken the sauce.

Dredging

Before dredging, rinse the chicken and pat thoroughly dry with paper towels. Spread flour on a plate or sheet of waxed paper, then press the chicken into the flour to coat all sides. Shake off any excess flour to ensure an attractive, evenly browned crust.

Browning

In a nonstick skillet, cook the coated chicken over medium heat until lightly browned and crisp on both sides, turning once halfway through cooking time. Take care not to overcrowd the pan or the chicken will steam instead of brown.

Skimming Fat

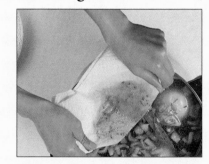

When simmering soup or stock, or preparing a sauce, from time to time lay a double thickness of paper towels on top to blot up fat. Or, to degrease a finished sauce, let it stand for a few minutes, then skim fat from the top with a wide, flat spoon.

SOUPS & SALADS

1

The vibrant mingling of sweet mango and spicy chili sauce, sharpened with a splash of lime juice, adds a Caribbean accent to this colorful salad. Make it up to a day ahead of time or serve it immediately. To cut preparation time as well as cleanup, microwave the sweet potato cubes, covered, at full power (100 percent) for four to five minutes, stirring once or twice.

Caribbean Chicken Salad

SERVES: 4
WORKING TIME: 15 MINUTES
TOTAL TIME: 25 MINUTES

¾ pound sweet potatoes, peeled and cut into 1-inch cubes

¾ cup chili sauce

¼ cup fresh lime juice

6 drops hot pepper sauce

1 pound skinless, boneless chicken breasts

1 cucumber, peeled, halved lengthwise, seeded, and diced

1 mango, halved, pitted, and cut into ½-inch pieces (see tip)

2 tablespoons minced scallion

1 tablespoon olive oil

3 cups ½-inch-wide shredded romaine lettuce

4 teaspoons coarsely chopped unsalted dry-roasted peanuts

1. In a medium saucepan, combine the sweet potatoes with water to cover. Bring to a boil over high heat, reduce to a simmer, cover, and cook until the potatoes are tender, about 10 minutes. Drain and cool.

2. Meanwhile, preheat the broiler. In a large bowl, combine the chili sauce, lime juice, and hot pepper sauce. Remove 3 tablespoons of this chili sauce mixture and set aside the remaining sauce. Place the chicken on the broiler rack and brush with the 3 tablespoons chili sauce mixture. Broil the chicken 4 inches from the heat for about 4 minutes per side, or until the chicken is just cooked through. Transfer the chicken to a cutting board and cut the chicken into thin diagonal slices.

3. Add the sweet potatoes, cucumber, mango, scallion, oil, and chicken slices to the reserved chili sauce mixture and toss to coat. Cover and refrigerate if not serving immediately.

4. Place the lettuce on 4 plates and spoon the chicken salad on top. Sprinkle with the peanuts and serve.

Suggested accompaniments: Sesame flat breads, and sliced bananas sprinkled with dark rum for dessert.

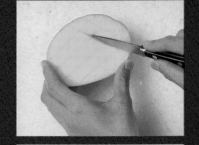

FAT: 7G/21%
CALORIES: 304
SATURATED FAT: 1.1G
CARBOHYDRATE: 32G
PROTEIN: 30G
CHOLESTEROL: 66MG
SODIUM: 423MG

Score each mango half into squares, cutting to, but not through, the skin. Turn the mango half inside out to pop the cut pieces outward. Cut the pieces away from the skin.

LOUISIANA-STYLE CHICKEN GUMBO

SERVES: 4
WORKING TIME: 25 MINUTES
TOTAL TIME: 35 MINUTES

A classic gumbo from the Mississippi Delta region begins with a fat-laden, flour-based roux that cooks for a considerable amount of time. This quicker version captures all the texture and spicy rich flavor of the original, but with much less fat.

⅓ cup long-grain rice

½ teaspoon salt

1 tablespoon olive oil

2 bell peppers, preferably 1 red and 1 green, diced

1⅓ cups diced celery

3 tablespoons flour

3 cups no-salt-added stewed tomatoes

2¼ cups reduced-sodium chicken broth, defatted

3 tablespoons no-salt-added tomato paste

1 teaspoon dried thyme

¾ teaspoon hot pepper sauce

10-ounce package frozen whole okra, thawed

¾ pound skinless, boneless chicken thighs, cut into 1-inch pieces

1. In a small saucepan, combine the rice, ⅔ cup of water, and ¼ teaspoon of the salt. Bring to a boil over high heat, reduce to a simmer, cover, and cook until the rice is tender, about 17 minutes.

2. Meanwhile, in a large saucepan, heat the oil until hot but not smoking over medium heat. Add the bell peppers and celery and cook, stirring frequently, until the vegetables are tender, about 5 minutes. Stir in the flour and cook, stirring constantly, until the flour is golden, about 4 minutes.

3. Stir in the tomatoes, breaking them up with the back of a spoon. Add the broth, tomato paste, thyme, hot pepper sauce, remaining ¼ teaspoon salt, and 1½ cups of water. Bring to a boil and cook for 5 minutes.

4. Stir in the okra and cook for 4 minutes. Add the chicken, reduce to a simmer, and cook until the chicken is cooked through and the okra is tender, about 7 minutes longer. Stir in the cooked rice, ladle the gumbo into 4 bowls, and serve.

Suggested accompaniment: Corn bread made with low-fat buttermilk instead of whole milk.

FAT: 8G/23%
CALORIES: 319
SATURATED FAT: 1.4G
CARBOHYDRATE: 41G
PROTEIN: 24G
CHOLESTEROL: 71MG
SODIUM: 811MG

15

LEMON-DILL CHICKEN AND RICE SOUP

SERVES: 4
WORKING TIME: 20 MINUTES
TOTAL TIME: 35 MINUTES

3 cups reduced-sodium chicken broth, defatted

1¾ pounds whole chicken legs, split and skinned

5 cloves garlic, minced

½ teaspoon salt

¾ cup long-grain rice

¾ cup diced leek or onion

4 carrots, thinly sliced

2 cups frozen lima beans or cut green beans

1 tablespoon fresh lemon juice

¼ cup chopped fresh dill, or 1 teaspoon dried

1. In a large saucepan, combine the broth, 4 cups of water, chicken, garlic, and salt. Bring to a boil over high heat, reduce to a simmer, cover, and cook until the chicken is cooked through, about 15 minutes. With a slotted spoon, transfer the chicken to a cutting board. Skim the fat from the broth.

2. Return the broth to a boil. Stir in the rice and leek, reduce to a simmer, cover, and cook for 10 minutes. Meanwhile, strip the chicken meat from the bones and dice the chicken.

3. Add the carrots, lima beans, and lemon juice to the broth and cook, uncovered, for 3 minutes. Stir in the diced chicken, cover, and simmer until the rice is tender, about 3 minutes longer. Stir in the dill, ladle the soup into 4 bowls, and serve. This soup is best served right away because the rice absorbs liquid on standing.

Suggested accompaniments: Sourdough baguette, and fresh orange wedges.

The flavorful partnership of lemon and dill adds a zesty twist to this country-kitchen favorite. If any soup is left over, add a little more broth when reheating since the rice will absorb liquid. Feel free to substitute chicken thighs or drumsticks for the whole legs.

FAT: 6G/13%
CALORIES: 414
SATURATED FAT: 1.3G
CARBOHYDRATE: 56G
PROTEIN: 33G
CHOLESTEROL: 91MG
SODIUM: 930MG

TACO SALAD WITH TOMATO-AVOCADO SALSA

SERVES: 4
WORKING TIME: 20 MINUTES
TOTAL TIME: 30 MINUTES

This festive salad boasts a potpourri of Southwestern flavors. The chicken and black bean mixture as well as the salsa can be prepared up to a day ahead and then arranged on plates before serving.

1 pound skinless, boneless chicken breasts

3 tablespoons fresh lime juice

½ teaspoon salt

Two 7-inch flour tortillas, each cut into 8 wedges

2¼ cups canned black beans, rinsed and drained

⅔ cup minced scallions

¾ teaspoon dried oregano

½ teaspoon ground cumin

1¼ pounds plum tomatoes (about 5), diced

¾ cup thinly sliced red onion

3 tablespoons chopped fresh basil, or 1 teaspoon dried

3 tablespoons red wine vinegar

⅓ cup diced avocado

4 cups coarsely torn romaine lettuce leaves

1. Preheat the broiler. Sprinkle the chicken with 1½ tablespoons of the lime juice and the salt. Place the chicken on the broiler rack and broil 4 inches from the heat for about 4 minutes per side, or until just cooked through. Transfer the chicken to a cutting board and cut the chicken into thin diagonal slices.

2. Turn the oven to 375°. Spread the tortilla wedges in a single layer on a nonstick baking sheet. Bake for 5 minutes, or until crisp and lightly toasted, rotating the baking sheet halfway through baking. Set aside to cool.

3. In a small bowl, combine the black beans, scallions, oregano, cumin, and remaining 1½ tablespoons lime juice. In a separate bowl, combine the tomatoes, red onion, basil, and vinegar and toss to combine. Gently stir in the avocado.

4. Place the lettuce on 4 plates and arrange the chicken slices on top. Place a mound of the black beans and a mound of the tomato-avocado salsa on each plate and serve with the toasted tortilla chips.

Suggested accompaniment: Raspberry sorbet for dessert.

FAT: 6G/15%
CALORIES: 353
SATURATED FAT: 1G
CARBOHYDRATE: 39G
PROTEIN: 37G
CHOLESTEROL: 66MG
SODIUM: 732MG

HEARTY CHICKEN AND CORN CHOWDER

SERVES: 4
WORKING TIME: 15 MINUTES
TOTAL TIME: 25 MINUTES

Creamed corn helps thicken this soup to a satisfying chowder consistency, without the added calories and fat of cream. When roadside farm stands are stacked high with sweet corn, certainly substitute freshly cooked corn off the cob for frozen in this chowder. For a variation, replace the parsley with fresh cilantro.

1 teaspoon olive oil
1 large onion, finely chopped
1 red bell pepper, diced
1 all-purpose potato, peeled and diced
1 ounce Canadian bacon, diced
1 cup reduced-sodium chicken broth, defatted
1 cup evaporated skimmed milk
1 cup canned creamed corn
¾ pound skinless, boneless chicken breasts, diced
½ teaspoon salt
¼ teaspoon freshly ground black pepper
¾ cup frozen corn kernels
2 tablespoons chopped fresh parsley

1. In a medium saucepan, heat the oil until hot but not smoking over medium heat. Add the onion, bell pepper, potato, and bacon. Cover and cook, stirring occasionally, until the vegetables begin to soften, about 5 minutes. Stir in the broth, evaporated milk, and creamed corn. Bring to a boil and reduce to a simmer. Cook, uncovered, stirring occasionally, for 10 minutes.

2. Stir in the diced chicken, salt, and black pepper and cook until the chicken is cooked through, about 5 minutes. Stir in the corn kernels and cook until the corn is just heated through, about 2 minutes longer. Ladle the chowder into 4 bowls, sprinkle with the parsley, and serve.

Suggested accompaniments: Green salad with a balsamic vinaigrette. For dessert, broiled peach halves topped with a little brown sugar.

FAT: 4G/12%
CALORIES: 296
SATURATED FAT: .8G
CARBOHYDRATE: 37G
PROTEIN: 31G
CHOLESTEROL: 57MG
SODIUM: 896MG

The sunny, assertive flavors of the Mediterranean are unmistakably at work in this salad: The sweetness of orange and honey is deliciously contrasted with the sharp and savory combination of red wine vinegar, mustard, and mint.

Mediterranean Chicken Salad

SERVES: 4
WORKING TIME: 25 MINUTES
TOTAL TIME: 30 MINUTES

3 slices (2 ounces each) crusty bread

1 clove garlic, peeled and halved

½ pound green beans, cut into 2-inch pieces

1 pound skinless, boneless chicken breasts

¾ teaspoon grated orange zest

1 cup orange juice

2 tablespoons honey

2 tablespoons red wine vinegar

1 tablespoon Dijon mustard

1 tablespoon olive oil

½ teaspoon salt

¾ pound plum tomatoes (about 3), cut into wedges

2 tablespoons chopped fresh mint

3 cups torn green-leaf lettuce leaves

1. Preheat the oven to 400°. Place the bread on a baking sheet and bake for 5 minutes, or until crisp and golden. Immediately rub the warm bread with the cut sides of the garlic (see tip). Cut the bread into small cubes for croutons. Set aside.

2. In a large pot of boiling water, cook the green beans until crisp-tender, about 2 minutes. Drain, rinse with cold water, and drain again.

3. In a large skillet, combine the chicken, orange zest, and orange juice. Bring to a boil over high heat, reduce to a simmer, cover, and cook until the chicken is cooked through, about 8 minutes. With a slotted spoon, transfer the chicken to a cutting board. Add the honey to the sauce, bring to a boil, and cook, uncovered, until reduced to ½ cup, about 5 minutes. Remove from the heat and cool slightly. Cut the chicken into thin diagonal slices.

4. In a large bowl, combine the cooled sauce, vinegar, mustard, oil, and salt. Add the green beans, tomatoes, mint, and chicken slices and toss to combine. Place the lettuce on 4 plates and spoon the chicken salad on top. Sprinkle with the croutons and serve.

Suggested accompaniments: Homemade limeade. Follow with assorted melon balls sprinkled with crushed macaroons and drizzled with honey.

FAT: 8G/22%
CALORIES: 322
SATURATED FAT: 1.3G
CARBOHYDRATE: 33G
PROTEIN: 30G
CHOLESTEROL: 66MG
SODIUM: 495MG

TIP

The garlic toast used for croutons in this salad contains none of the oil or butter of traditional garlic bread, but tastes just as good. Use this easy method whenever garlic bread is called for.

CHICKEN AND WHITE BEAN SALAD

SERVES: 4
WORKING TIME: 20 MINUTES
TOTAL TIME: 25 MINUTES

Serve this picture-perfect salad for a lovely lunch or light summer supper. Soaking the onion in ice water removes its bitterness.

½ cup chopped red onion

1 pound skinless, boneless chicken breasts, cut into ½-inch-thick strips

1 cup reduced-sodium chicken broth, defatted

1 cup plain nonfat yogurt

2 tablespoons reduced-fat mayonnaise

½ teaspoon salt

¼ teaspoon freshly ground black pepper

16-ounce can white kidney beans, rinsed and drained

2 tomatoes, diced

2 cucumbers, peeled, halved lengthwise, seeded, and diced

⅓ cup chopped fresh dill

3 tablespoons fresh lemon juice

2 teaspoons olive oil

4 cups ¼-inch-wide shredded romaine lettuce

1. In a small bowl, combine the red onion with ice water to cover and let stand for 10 minutes.

2. Meanwhile, in a large skillet, combine the chicken and broth. Bring to a boil over high heat, reduce to a simmer, cover, and cook until the chicken is cooked through, about 5 minutes. With a slotted spoon, transfer the chicken to a plate and set aside. Return the broth to a boil and cook, uncovered, until reduced to ⅓ cup, about 5 minutes. Remove the broth from the heat and cool slightly. Skim the fat from the broth.

3. In a large bowl, combine the yogurt, mayonnaise, cooled broth, salt, and pepper. Add the chicken and toss well to coat. Drain the red onion, pat dry with paper towels, and add to the chicken mixture. Gently stir in the kidney beans, tomatoes, cucumbers, and half of the dill. Cover and refrigerate if not serving immediately.

4. In a medium bowl, whisk together the lemon juice, oil, and remaining dill. Add the lettuce and toss to coat. Spoon the lettuce mixture onto 4 plates, spoon the chicken salad on top, and serve.

Suggested accompaniments: Seven-grain bread, and thin slices of part-skim mozzarella cheese.

FAT: 8G/21%
CALORIES: 342
SATURATED FAT: 1.8G
CARBOHYDRATE: 30G
PROTEIN: 38G
CHOLESTEROL: 72MG
SODIUM: 752MG

ORIENTAL CHICKEN SOUP

SERVES: 4
WORKING TIME: 15 MINUTES
TOTAL TIME: 25 MINUTES

2 cups reduced-sodium chicken broth, defatted

1¼ pounds whole chicken legs, split and skinned

2 cloves garlic, minced

2 red bell peppers, diced

3 tablespoons cider vinegar

1 tablespoon reduced-sodium soy sauce

¾ teaspoon ground ginger

¼ teaspoon salt

3 cups ½-inch-wide shredded cabbage

3 ounces capellini noodles, broken into small pieces

¼ pound snow peas, cut into ½-inch diagonal pieces

2 scallions, finely chopped

¼ pound firm tofu, cut into ½-inch chunks

¼ teaspoon sesame oil

1. In a medium saucepan, combine the broth, 3½ cups of water, chicken, and garlic. Bring to a boil over high heat, reduce to a simmer, cover, and cook until the chicken is cooked through, about 15 minutes. With a slotted spoon, transfer the chicken to a cutting board. Strip the chicken meat from the bones and dice the chicken. Skim the fat from the broth.

2. Return the broth to a boil. Add the bell peppers, vinegar, soy sauce, ginger, and salt and cook for 2 minutes. Stir in the cabbage, capellini, snow peas, scallions, diced chicken, and more water to cover, if necessary. Cook until the capellini is tender, about 2 minutes longer. Stir in the tofu and sesame oil, ladle the soup into 4 bowls, and serve.

Suggested accompaniments: Thin bread sticks, and chilled red and green seedless grapes.

FAT: 7G/23%
CALORIES: 274
SATURATED FAT: 1.2G
CARBOHYDRATE: 27G
PROTEIN: 27G
CHOLESTEROL: 64MG
SODIUM: 693MG

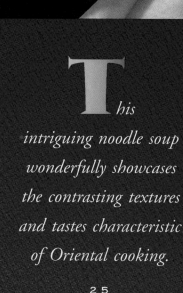

This intriguing noodle soup wonderfully showcases the contrasting textures and tastes characteristic of Oriental cooking.

Watercress and water chestnuts add crunch and pepperiness to this Mediterranean-inspired salad, while the broiled, herb-coated chicken breasts and bell pepper lend a smoky flavor. If weather permits, grill the chicken and the pepper outdoors.

BROILED CHICKEN AND ORANGE SALAD

SERVES: 4
WORKING TIME: 25 MINUTES
TOTAL TIME: 30 MINUTES

¾ teaspoon dried oregano

½ teaspoon ground cumin

½ teaspoon dried rosemary

½ teaspoon salt

1 pound skinless, boneless chicken breasts

1 yellow or red bell pepper, halved

2 tablespoons cider vinegar

1 tablespoon low-sodium ketchup

1 teaspoon vegetable oil

⅛ teaspoon cayenne pepper

8-ounce can sliced water chestnuts, rinsed and drained

3 navel oranges, peeled and sectioned

1 bunch watercress (about 6 ounces), thick stems trimmed

1 tablespoon coarsely chopped pecans

1. Preheat the broiler. In a cup, combine ½ teaspoon of the oregano, ¼ teaspoon of the cumin, the rosemary, and salt. Rub the chicken with the herb mixture.

2. Place the chicken and the bell pepper halves, cut-sides down, on the broiler rack. Broil the chicken 4 inches from the heat for about 4 minutes per side, or until just cooked through. Transfer the chicken to a cutting board. Continue to broil the pepper halves for 4 minutes longer, or until the skin is blackened (see tip). Transfer the pepper halves to a small bowl, cover with plastic wrap, and let stand for 5 minutes.

3. Meanwhile, cut the chicken into diagonal slices. Transfer the pepper halves to the cutting board. Remove the peel from the peppers, remove any seeds, and cut the peppers into thin strips.

4. In a medium bowl, combine the vinegar, ketchup, oil, cayenne, remaining ¼ teaspoon oregano, and remaining ¼ teaspoon cumin. Add the pepper strips, water chestnuts, orange sections, and watercress and toss to coat. Place the watercress-orange salad on 4 plates and arrange the chicken slices on top. Sprinkle with the pecans and serve.

Suggested accompaniments: Whole-grain rolls and, for dessert, peach nonfat yogurt sprinkled with fresh blueberries.

FAT: 4G/15%
CALORIES: 238
SATURATED FAT: .6G
CARBOHYDRATE: 23G
PROTEIN: 29G
CHOLESTEROL: 66MG
SODIUM: 259MG

TIP

The skin of broiled or roasted bell peppers can be removed easily by grasping the blackened skin and pulling it away from the flesh.

CREAMY CHICKEN SOUP WITH VEGETABLES

SERVES: 4
WORKING TIME: 15 MINUTES
TOTAL TIME: 30 MINUTES

3 cups reduced-sodium chicken broth, defatted

1¼ pounds whole chicken legs, split and skinned

3 cloves garlic, peeled

¼ teaspoon salt

4 ribs celery, diced

1 yellow summer squash (about 10 ounces), thinly sliced

1 cup evaporated skimmed milk

3 tablespoons cornstarch

1½ cups frozen peas

1. In a large saucepan, combine the broth, 1 cup of water, chicken, garlic, and salt. Bring to a boil over high heat, reduce to a simmer, cover, and cook until the chicken is cooked through, about 15 minutes. With a slotted spoon, transfer the chicken and garlic to a cutting board. Strip the chicken meat from the bones and dice the chicken. Discard the garlic.

2. Add the celery, squash, and evaporated milk to the broth. Return to a boil and cook until the vegetables are tender, about 3 minutes. In a cup, combine the cornstarch and 2 tablespoons of water, stir to blend, and stir into the boiling soup along with the diced chicken and peas. Reduce to a simmer and cook, stirring constantly, until the soup is slightly thickened and the peas are heated through, about 3 minutes longer. Ladle the soup into 4 bowls and serve.

Suggested accompaniments: Apple cider, and a roasted red pepper salad with a lemon dressing.

Whole garlic cloves simmered with chicken richly flavor this soup, while evaporated skimmed milk provides creaminess without excess fat. You may substitute zucchini for the yellow squash and lima beans for the peas. Serve steaming mugs of this soup for a pick-me-up on a chilly winter afternoon.

FAT: 4G/15%
CALORIES: 246
SATURATED FAT: .9G
CARBOHYDRATE: 25G
PROTEIN: 26G
CHOLESTEROL: 67MG
SODIUM: 846MG

CHICKEN AND POTATO SALAD

SERVES: 4
WORKING TIME: 20 MINUTES
TOTAL TIME: 35 MINUTES

A picnic side-dish favorite elevated to a substantial main-dish role, this flavorful potato salad features broth-poached chicken, bell peppers, and a hint of smoky Canadian bacon. For a decorative touch, garnish the salad with sprigs of fresh rosemary.

1 pound skinless, boneless chicken breasts

1 pound small red potatoes, cut into ½-inch pieces

1½ cups reduced-sodium chicken broth, defatted

½ cup plain nonfat yogurt

2 tablespoons white wine vinegar

1 tablespoon light sour cream

1 tablespoon Dijon mustard

2 teaspoons reduced-fat mayonnaise

2 teaspoons chopped fresh rosemary, or ½ teaspoon dried

½ teaspoon salt

1 red bell pepper, diced

1 green bell pepper, diced

1 medium red onion, minced

1 ounce Canadian bacon, diced

1. In a large nonstick skillet, combine the chicken, potatoes, and broth. Bring to a boil over high heat, reduce to a simmer, cover, and cook until the chicken and the potatoes are cooked through, about 10 minutes. With a slotted spoon, transfer the chicken and potatoes to a cutting board. Skim the fat from the broth.

2. Return the broth to a boil and cook, uncovered, until reduced to ¼ cup, about 5 minutes. Remove the broth from the heat and cool slightly. Cut the chicken into 1½-inch chunks.

3. In a large bowl, combine the yogurt, vinegar, sour cream, mustard, mayonnaise, cooled broth, rosemary, and salt. Add the bell peppers, onion, bacon, chicken, and potatoes and toss to coat. Place the chicken salad on 4 plates and serve.

Suggested accompaniments: Bread sticks or crusty French bread, and fresh apple wedges.

FAT: 4G/13%
CALORIES: 275
SATURATED FAT: 1G
CARBOHYDRATE: 25G
PROTEIN: 33G
CHOLESTEROL: 72MG
SODIUM: 843MG

CHINESE CHICKEN SALAD WITH PEANUTS

SERVES: 4
WORKING TIME: 15 MINUTES
TOTAL TIME: 20 MINUTES

The hoisin sauce and apple juice create both a sharp-sweet dressing for this salad and a quick marinade for the chicken breasts. For a peppery variation, substitute alfalfa or radish sprouts for the bean sprouts.

⅓ cup hoisin sauce

¼ cup apple juice

1 teaspoon vegetable oil

¼ teaspoon salt

1 pound skinless, boneless chicken breasts

2 red bell peppers, cut into thin strips

2 carrots, shredded

2 cups bean sprouts

8-ounce can sliced water chestnuts, rinsed and drained

2 tablespoons finely chopped scallion

½ teaspoon ground ginger

3 cups ¼-inch-wide shredded romaine lettuce

1 tablespoon coarsely chopped unsalted dry-roasted peanuts

1. Preheat the broiler. In a large bowl, combine the hoisin sauce, apple juice, oil, and salt. Remove 2 tablespoons of this hoisin sauce mixture and set aside the remaining sauce. Place the chicken on the broiler rack and brush with the 2 tablespoons hoisin sauce mixture. Broil the chicken 4 inches from the heat for 4 minutes per side, or until just cooked through. Transfer the chicken to a cutting board and cut the chicken into thin diagonal slices.

2. Add the chicken slices, bell pepper strips, carrots, sprouts, water chestnuts, scallion, and ginger to the reserved hoisin sauce mixture and toss to coat.

3. Place the lettuce on 4 plates and spoon the chicken salad on top. Sprinkle with the peanuts and serve.

Suggested accompaniments: Rice cakes, and oolong or almond tea with fortune cookies afterward.

FAT: 4G/13%
CALORIES: 275
SATURATED FAT: .7G
CARBOHYDRATE: 29G
PROTEIN: 31G
CHOLESTEROL: 66MG
SODIUM: 914MG

CHICKEN AND WINTER VEGETABLE SOUP

SERVES: 4
WORKING TIME: 20 MINUTES
TOTAL TIME: 30 MINUTES

4 cups reduced-sodium chicken broth, defatted

1¼ pounds whole chicken legs, split and skinned

3 cloves garlic, minced

½ teaspoon dried marjoram

¼ teaspoon salt

2 leeks, white and light green parts only, diced

¾ pound all-purpose potatoes, peeled and cut into ½-inch dice

1 turnip, cut into ½-inch dice

1 parsnip, cut into ½-inch dice (about ¾ cup)

1 large onion, diced

10 ounces green beans, cut into 2-inch pieces (about 2 cups)

¾ pound plum tomatoes (about 3), diced

2 tablespoons chopped fresh parsley

1. In a large saucepan, combine the broth, 2 cups of water, chicken, garlic, marjoram, and salt. Bring to a boil over high heat, reduce to a simmer, cover, and cook until the chicken is cooked through, about 15 minutes. With a slotted spoon, transfer the chicken to a cutting board. Strip the chicken meat from the bones and dice the chicken. Skim the fat from the broth.

2. Return the broth to a boil. Add the leeks, potatoes, turnip, parsnip, and onion, reduce to a simmer, cover, and cook until the vegetables are almost tender, about 5 minutes. Stir in the beans and tomatoes and cook, uncovered, until the beans are tender, about 5 minutes longer. Ladle the soup into 4 bowls, sprinkle with the parsley, and serve.

Suggested accompaniments: Shredded carrot salad with a light sour cream dressing, and reduced-fat vanilla pudding sprinkled with crumbled vanilla wafers for dessert.

Ideal for colder months, this version of a classic spotlights root vegetables: turnips, parsnips, and potatoes. If good-quality plum tomatoes are not available, use one and one-half cups of drained canned whole tomatoes, chopped. For extra zip, substitute minced scallion greens for the parsley garnish.

FAT: 5G/16%
CALORIES: 280
SATURATED FAT: .9G
CARBOHYDRATE: 38G
PROTEIN: 23G
CHOLESTEROL: 64MG
SODIUM: 899MG

This refreshing bulghur salad with its cool tastes of mint, scallion, and lemon juice is a favorite for sultry summer days. We've kept our version of this salad low in fat by replacing the oil with a dressing made from lemon juice and chicken broth. Because the lemon juice plays such an important role in this recipe, it's especially important to use fresh-squeezed.

CHICKEN TABBOULEH SALAD

SERVES: 4
WORKING TIME: 15 MINUTES
TOTAL TIME: 35 MINUTES

⅔ cup bulghur (cracked wheat)

2 cups boiling water

1 pound skinless, boneless chicken breasts

¼ cup plus 2 tablespoons fresh lemon juice

⅓ cup reduced-sodium chicken broth, defatted

½ teaspoon cornstarch

16-ounce can chick-peas, rinsed and drained

⅓ cup minced scallion

3 tablespoons chopped fresh parsley

2 tablespoons chopped fresh mint

¾ teaspoon salt

½ teaspoon allspice

¾ pound plum tomatoes (about 3), diced

1. In a medium bowl, combine the bulghur and boiling water. Let stand until the bulghur has softened, about 30 minutes. Drain and squeeze dry (see tip).

2. Meanwhile, preheat the broiler. Place the chicken on the broiler rack and brush with 2 tablespoons of the lemon juice. Broil the chicken 4 inches from the heat about 4 minutes per side, or until just cooked through. Transfer the chicken to a cutting board and cut the chicken into thin diagonal slices.

3. In a small saucepan, combine the broth and the remaining ¼ cup lemon juice. Bring to a boil over high heat. In a cup, combine the cornstarch and 2 teaspoons of cold water, stir to blend, and stir into the boiling broth. Cook until slightly thickened, stirring constantly, about 1 minute. Remove from the heat and cool slightly.

4. In a large bowl, combine the drained bulghur, chick-peas, scallion, parsley, mint, salt, and allspice. Add the tomatoes and toss gently to combine. Spoon the bulghur mixture onto 4 plates and arrange the chicken slices on top. Drizzle with the cooled lemon dressing and serve.

Suggested accompaniments: Iced tea with mint, and fresh pineapple spears.

FAT: 4G/12%
CALORIES: 312
SATURATED FAT: .5G
CARBOHYDRATE: 36G
PROTEIN: 34G
CHOLESTEROL: 66MG
SODIUM: 676MG

TIP

Bulghur, or cracked wheat, can be prepared very quickly since the wheat berries have already been steamed, then dried and cracked into coarse, medium, or fine grinds. Combine the bulghur with boiling water and let stand until softened. Drain in a fine-mesh sieve, and then, with your hands, squeeze the bulghur dry.

Mom's Chicken Noodle Soup

Serves: 4
Working time: 15 minutes
Total time: 35 minutes

Sure to chase the chill from a winter evening, this simple soup encourages variations. Try substituting turnips or potatoes for the parsnips, and other shapes, such as rotelle, fusilli, or ditalini, for the pasta shells.

3 cups reduced-sodium chicken broth, defatted

1¼ pounds whole chicken legs, split and skinned

3 cloves garlic, peeled

¼ teaspoon salt

2 medium onions, diced

2 carrots, thinly sliced

2 parsnips, thinly sliced (about 1½ cups)

2 ribs celery, thinly sliced

4 ounces small pasta shells

2 tablespoons chopped fresh dill

1. In a large saucepan, combine the broth, 2 cups of water, chicken, garlic, and salt. Bring to a boil over high heat, reduce to a simmer, cover, and cook until the chicken is cooked through, about 15 minutes. With a slotted spoon, transfer the chicken and garlic to a cutting board. Strip the chicken meat from the bones and dice the chicken. Discard the garlic. Skim the fat from the broth.

2. Add the onions, carrots, parsnips, and celery to the broth. Return to a boil, reduce to a simmer, cover, and cook until the vegetables are almost tender, about 5 minutes. Stir in the pasta and cook, uncovered, for 7 minutes. Add the diced chicken and cook until the pasta is tender, about 3 minutes longer. Stir in the dill, ladle the soup into 4 bowls, and serve.

Suggested accompaniments: Crusty rolls, and a tossed green salad with an herbed buttermilk dressing.

Fat: 5g/15%
Calories: 307
Saturated Fat: .9g
Carbohydrate: 42g
Protein: 24g
Cholesterol: 64mg
Sodium: 737mg

New Deli Chicken Salad

SERVES: 4
WORKING TIME: 15 MINUTES
TOTAL TIME: 25 MINUTES

The delicious dressing for this updated deli salad features nonfat yogurt with just a touch of reduced-fat mayonnaise to soften the yogurt's sharpness. Refrigerate the chicken mixture for a day and the flavors will be even better. To shred the chicken, pull it into long, thin pieces, following the grain of the meat.

1 pound skinless, boneless chicken breasts

½ teaspoon dried thyme

½ teaspoon salt

½ cup plain nonfat yogurt

2 tablespoons low-sodium ketchup

1 tablespoon reduced-fat mayonnaise

2 teaspoons Dijon mustard

⅛ teaspoon freshly ground black pepper

2 ribs celery, diced

1 red onion, minced

1 cucumber, peeled, halved lengthwise, seeded, and diced

¼ cup diced sweet gherkins

3 tablespoons chopped black olives (optional)

12 leaves romaine lettuce

2 tomatoes, each cut into 8 wedges

1. Preheat the broiler. Rub the chicken with the thyme and salt. Place the chicken on the broiler rack and broil 4 inches from the heat about 4 minutes per side, or until just cooked through. Transfer the chicken to a cutting board. When cool enough to handle, coarsely shred the chicken.

2. In a medium bowl, combine the yogurt, ketchup, mayonnaise, mustard, and pepper. Add the celery, onion, cucumber, gherkins, and olives and toss to coat. Add the shredded chicken and mix well.

3. Place the lettuce on 4 plates and spoon the chicken salad on top. Arrange 4 tomato wedges on each plate and serve.

Suggested accompaniments: Bagel crisps and, for dessert, parfait glasses of vanilla nonfat yogurt layered with fresh cherries.

FAT: 3G/12%
CALORIES: 232
SATURATED FAT: .7G
CARBOHYDRATE: 20G
PROTEIN: 30G
CHOLESTEROL: 68MG
SODIUM: 655MG

CHICKEN COBB SALAD

SERVES: 4
WORKING TIME: 15 MINUTES
TOTAL TIME: 20 MINUTES

*T*he secret ingredient here is mango chutney, which pairs beautifully with the tart apple. Piquant blue cheese is the Cobb salad signature.

1 pound skinless, boneless chicken breasts

⅔ cup plain nonfat yogurt

3 tablespoons mango chutney

2 tablespoons reduced-fat mayonnaise

1 tablespoon fresh lemon juice

½ teaspoon salt

2 apples, preferably 1 Granny Smith and 1 McIntosh, cored and diced

1 rib celery, finely diced

2 tablespoons minced scallion

12 leaves Boston lettuce

1 ounce blue cheese, crumbled

1. Preheat the broiler. Place the chicken on the broiler rack and broil 4 inches from the heat for about 4 minutes per side, or until just cooked through. Transfer the chicken to a cutting board and cut the chicken into ¾-inch chunks.

2. In a large bowl, combine the yogurt, chutney, mayonnaise, lemon juice, and salt and stir to blend. Add the apples, celery, and scallion. Fold in the chicken until well coated.

3. Arrange the lettuce leaves on 4 plates and spoon the chicken salad on top. Sprinkle with the blue cheese and serve.

Suggested accompaniments: Dark pumpernickel bread, and fresh fruit.

FAT: 6G/20%
CALORIES: 268
SATURATED FAT: 2.2G
CARBOHYDRATE: 22G
PROTEIN: 30G
CHOLESTEROL: 74MG
SODIUM: 654MG

BRAISES & STEWS

2

SAVORY CHICKEN, CARROT, AND POTATO STEW

SERVES: 4
WORKING TIME: 20 MINUTES
TOTAL TIME: 40 MINUTES

*T*he flavors of garlic and rosemary enliven this hearty knife-and-fork stew, while carrots and peas add delightful splashes of color. A quick pre-browning in the pan keeps the drumsticks extra juicy. Make sure to use the full amount of garlic cloves because their pungency diminishes with cooking time.

2 tablespoons flour
½ teaspoon salt
¼ teaspoon freshly ground black pepper
8 chicken drumsticks (about 2 pounds total), skinned
1 tablespoon vegetable oil
10 cloves garlic, peeled
4 carrots, thinly sliced
2 bunches scallions, cut into 2-inch lengths
1½ pounds small red potatoes, thinly sliced
1½ teaspoons dried rosemary
1 cup dry white wine
2 cups reduced-sodium chicken broth, defatted
1½ cups frozen peas

1. On a plate, combine the flour, ¼ teaspoon of the salt, and the pepper. Dredge the chicken in the flour mixture, shaking off the excess. In a nonstick Dutch oven, heat the oil until hot but not smoking over medium heat. Add the chicken and cook until golden brown on all sides, about 5 minutes. Transfer the chicken to a plate.

2. Add the garlic, carrots, scallions, potatoes, rosemary, and the remaining ¼ teaspoon salt to the pan and cook, stirring frequently, until the vegetables begin to brown, about 5 minutes. Add the wine and cook for 3 minutes. Return the chicken to the pan and add the broth. Bring to a boil over medium-high heat, reduce to a simmer, and cover. Cook, turning the chicken occasionally, until the chicken is cooked through and the vegetables are tender, about 15 minutes.

3. Stir in the peas and cook, uncovered, until the peas are heated through, about 3 minutes longer. Spoon the stew into 4 bowls and serve.

Suggested accompaniments: Crusty rolls, followed by Bartlett or Anjou pear halves poached in a vanilla sugar syrup for dessert.

FAT: 9G/17%
CALORIES: 487
SATURATED FAT: 1.6G
CARBOHYDRATE: 57G
PROTEIN: 35G
CHOLESTEROL: 94MG
SODIUM: 683MG

*T*he aroma of the sweet Middle Eastern mixture of ginger and cinnamon will perfume the kitchen as the chicken simmers in its savory broth. For this simple twist on the classic Moroccan stew, we've used quick-cooking couscous, a pasta that requires just a few minutes of steeping in the hot broth or other liquid.

SPICED CHICKEN COUSCOUS

SERVES: 4
WORKING TIME: 15 MINUTES
TOTAL TIME: 20 MINUTES

3 cups reduced-sodium chicken broth, defatted

1½ teaspoons ground cumin

1 teaspoon turmeric

1 teaspoon ground ginger

1 teaspoon cinnamon

½ teaspoon freshly ground black pepper

8 drops hot pepper sauce

1⅓ cups couscous

1½ teaspoons fresh lemon juice

1 pound skinless, boneless chicken thighs, cut into 1½-inch chunks

3 zucchini, cut into 3-inch-long strips

2 carrots, cut into 3-inch-long strips

¼ cup dark raisins

3 tablespoons blanched slivered almonds, toasted

1. In a large saucepan, combine the broth, 1½ cups of water, the cumin, turmeric, ginger, cinnamon, black pepper, and hot pepper sauce. Bring to a boil over high heat and cook for 3 minutes.

2. In a medium bowl, combine the couscous and lemon juice. Transfer 1 cup of the boiling broth to the bowl, cover, and let stand until the couscous has softened, about 5 minutes.

3. Meanwhile, add the chicken, zucchini, carrots, and more water to cover, if necessary, to the remaining broth. Return to a boil, reduce to a simmer, cover, and cook until the chicken is cooked through, about 5 minutes.

4. Fluff the couscous with a fork (see tip) and spoon onto 4 serving plates. With a slotted spoon, remove the chicken and vegetables from the broth, place on top of the couscous, and sprinkle with the raisins and almonds. Pour the broth into a sauceboat and serve along with the stew.

Suggested accompaniments: Toasted pita bread, and a Bibb lettuce salad with a citrus vinaigrette.

FAT: 9G/17%
CALORIES: 488
SATURATED FAT: 1.6G
CARBOHYDRATE: 66G
PROTEIN: 35G
CHOLESTEROL: 94MG
SODIUM: 609MG

TIP

Traditional North African couscous is fine-grained cracked semolina, which takes a long time and quite a bit of fussing to prepare. But the couscous found in supermarkets is a precooked semolina pasta that requires only steeping. Use a fork to fluff the softened couscous, which will separate the grains without crushing them.

CHICKEN AND APPLES NORMANDY

SERVES: 4
WORKING TIME: 20 MINUTES
TOTAL TIME: 30 MINUTES

2 Granny Smith apples, cored and chopped

2 red bell peppers, cut into ½-inch chunks

1 large onion, chopped

1½ cups apple cider or natural apple juice

¼ cup cider vinegar

¾ teaspoon salt

1 tablespoon flour

¼ teaspoon freshly ground black pepper

4 skinless, boneless chicken breast halves (about 1 pound total)

2 teaspoons olive oil

3 tablespoons light sour cream

1. In a medium saucepan, combine the apples, bell peppers, onion, apple cider, vinegar, and ½ teaspoon of the salt. Bring to a boil over high heat, reduce to a simmer, and cook, partially covered, until the apples and vegetables begin to soften, about 7 minutes.

2. Meanwhile, on a plate, combine the flour, black pepper, and the remaining ¼ teaspoon salt. Dredge the chicken in the flour mixture, shaking off the excess. In a large nonstick skillet, heat the oil until hot but not smoking over medium heat. Add the chicken and cook, turning once, until golden brown, about 5 minutes. Add the apple mixture and bring to a boil over medium-high heat. Reduce to a simmer, cover, and cook until the chicken is cooked through, about 10 minutes longer.

3. With a slotted spoon, transfer the chicken to 4 serving plates. Stir the sour cream into the apple mixture, spoon over the chicken, and serve.

Suggested accompaniments: Wide noodles. For dessert, a reduced-calorie lemon pudding garnished with chopped crystallized ginger.

Tart apples and silky sour cream create a richly mellow sauce for this chicken. To make the dish nutritionally sensible without affecting the luscious flavor, we've used light sour cream and skinless chicken breasts. Be sure to serve over noodles or rice to soak up every bit of this delectable sauce.

FAT: 6G/19%
CALORIES: 284
SATURATED FAT: 1.5G
CARBOHYDRATE: 31G
PROTEIN: 28G
CHOLESTEROL: 70MG
SODIUM: 491MG

OVEN-BRAISED ROSEMARY CHICKEN WITH VEGETABLES

SERVES: 4
WORKING TIME: 20 MINUTES
TOTAL TIME: 50 MINUTES

Sun-dried tomatoes elegantly update this country dish. And all the cooking is done in one roasting pan in the oven.

1 tablespoon olive oil

3 cloves garlic, unpeeled

2 parsnips, thinly sliced (about 1½ cups)

2 medium onions, cut into 1-inch chunks

¾ pound sweet potatoes, peeled and thinly sliced

2 cups cut butternut squash (1-inch cubes)

6 sprigs fresh rosemary, or 4 teaspoons dried

½ teaspoon mild paprika

½ teaspoon salt

½ cup sun-dried (not oil-packed) tomato halves, coarsely chopped

⅔ cup boiling water

4 bone-in chicken breast halves (about 1½ pounds total), skinned

¼ teaspoon freshly ground black pepper

1. Preheat the oven to 400°. In a large roasting pan, combine the oil, garlic, parsnips, onions, sweet potatoes, squash, 2 sprigs of the rosemary or 1 teaspoon of the dried, the paprika, and ¼ teaspoon of the salt. Cover with foil and bake for 20 minutes, or until the vegetables begin to soften.

2. Meanwhile, in a small bowl, combine the sun-dried tomatoes and the boiling water. Let stand until the tomatoes have softened, about 10 minutes.

3. Sprinkle the chicken with the remaining ¼ teaspoon salt and the pepper and place on top of the vegetables. Add the sun-dried tomatoes and their soaking liquid and the remaining rosemary. Bake for 20 minutes longer, or until the vegetables are tender and the chicken is cooked through. Spoon the chicken and vegetables onto 4 plates and serve.

Suggested accompaniments: Caraway rye bread, and a light dessert of stewed dried apricots, pears, and cherries.

FAT: 6G/16%
CALORIES: 347
SATURATED FAT: 1G
CARBOHYDRATE: 45G
PROTEIN: 31G
CHOLESTEROL: 65MG
SODIUM: 378MG

Chicken in Red Wine Sauce

Serves: 4
Working time: 20 minutes
Total time: 45 minutes

2 teaspoons olive oil

1 ounce Canadian bacon, diced

2 tablespoons flour

½ teaspoon salt

¼ teaspoon freshly ground black pepper

8 skinless, boneless chicken thighs (about 1½ pounds total)

4 carrots, cut into 1-inch pieces

2 large onions, cut into 1-inch chunks

1½ pounds small red potatoes, cut into 1-inch chunks

1⅓ cups dry red wine

1 cup reduced-sodium chicken broth, defatted

2 tablespoons no-salt-added tomato paste

2 cups frozen peas

1. In a nonstick Dutch oven, heat the oil until hot but not smoking over medium heat. Add the bacon and cook until lightly crisped, about 4 minutes. With a slotted spoon, transfer the bacon to a plate.

2. On a separate plate, combine the flour, ¼ teaspoon of the salt, and the pepper. Dredge the chicken in the flour mixture, shaking off the excess. Heat the drippings remaining in the pan over medium heat. Add the chicken and cook until golden brown on all sides, about 5 minutes. Transfer the chicken to the plate with the bacon.

3. Add the carrots, onions, potatoes, and 1 cup of water to the pan and cook over low heat, stirring occasionally, for 5 minutes. Add the wine, increase the heat to high, and cook for 3 minutes. Stir in the broth, tomato paste, and remaining ¼ teaspoon salt. Return the bacon and chicken to the pan. Bring to a boil, reduce to a simmer, cover, and cook until the vegetables are tender and the chicken is cooked through, about 12 minutes.

4. Stir in the peas and cook, uncovered, until the peas are heated through, about 3 minutes longer. Spoon the chicken mixture into 4 bowls and serve.

Suggested accompaniments: Spinach salad with goat cheese and a balsamic vinaigrette, followed by fresh strawberries drizzled with orange liqueur.

Fat: 12g/17%
Calories: 625
Saturated Fat: 2.5g
Carbohydrate: 72g
Protein: 46g
Cholesterol: 145mg
Sodium: 811mg

*T*his *French-style classic is chunky with vegetables. For best flavor, don't skimp on the quality of the red wine.*

51

This
tantalizing dish
creatively matches
sweet butternut squash
with mildly nutty
artichoke hearts. You
may substitute acorn
squash or sweet
dumpling squash for
the butternut. To make
the stew a day ahead,
follow the recipe,
omitting the peas.
Cover and refrigerate.
To serve, add the peas
and reheat gently on
the stovetop.

CHICKEN WITH WINTER SQUASH AND ARTICHOKES

Serves: 4
Working time: 25 minutes
Total time: 40 minutes

1 tablespoon flour

½ teaspoon salt

¼ teaspoon freshly ground black pepper

4 skinless, boneless chicken breast halves (about 1 pound total)

2 teaspoons olive oil

4½ cups cut butternut squash (¾-inch cubes; see tip)

1 tablespoon sugar

10-ounce package frozen artichoke hearts, thawed

2 scallions, minced

3 tablespoons chopped fresh parsley

2 tablespoons fresh lemon juice

¾ teaspoon dried marjoram

1½ cups frozen peas

1. On a plate, combine the flour, ¼ teaspoon of the salt, and the pepper. Dredge the chicken in the flour mixture, shaking off the excess. In a large nonstick skillet, heat the oil until hot but not smoking over medium heat. Add the chicken and cook, turning once, until golden brown, about 5 minutes. Transfer the chicken to a plate.

2. Add the squash to the pan, sprinkle with the sugar, and cook, stirring frequently, until the squash is lightly browned, about 5 minutes. Add the artichoke hearts, scallions, parsley, lemon juice, marjoram, 1 cup of water, and the remaining ¼ teaspoon salt and bring to a boil. Return the chicken to the pan, reduce to a simmer, cover, and cook until the artichokes are tender and the chicken is cooked through, about 12 minutes.

3. Stir in the peas and cook, uncovered, until the peas are heated through, about 3 minutes longer. Spoon the chicken and vegetables onto 4 plates and serve.

Suggested accompaniments: Basmati rice with diced red bell peppers. For dessert, drizzle fresh figs with honey.

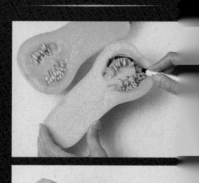

To prepare squash, halve it lengthwise, scoop out the seeds, and peel. Cut the squash halves lengthwise into ¾-inch-wide pieces, then cut crosswise into uniform ¾-inch cubes.

Fat: 4G/12%
Calories: 303
Saturated Fat: .8G
Carbohydrate: 36G
Protein: 33G
Cholesterol: 66MG
Sodium: 449MG

CHUNKY CHICKEN AND CORN CHILI

SERVES: 4
WORKING TIME: 15 MINUTES
TOTAL TIME: 25 MINUTES

To add rich flavor to this robust chili, we've first cooked the fragrant spices in a little oil. And, to reduce the sodium content, we've rinsed the beans and used no-salt-added tomato sauce. Dark meat chicken makes a particularly flavorful chili, but skinless white meat chicken may be substituted.

2 teaspoons vegetable oil
2 large onions, coarsely chopped
6 cloves garlic, minced
1½ tablespoons mild chili powder
1½ teaspoons dried oregano
1 teaspoon ground cumin
1 teaspoon ground coriander
1 teaspoon cinnamon
¾ teaspoon freshly ground black pepper
½ teaspoon salt
1 pound skinless, boneless chicken thighs, cut into ½-inch chunks
Two 8-ounce cans no-salt-added tomato sauce
Two 16-ounce cans kidney beans, rinsed and drained
2 cups frozen corn kernels
2 tablespoons light sour cream

1. In a nonstick Dutch oven, heat the oil until hot but not smoking over medium heat. Add the onions and garlic and cook, stirring frequently, until the onions begin to soften, about 5 minutes. Stir in the chili powder, oregano, cumin, coriander, cinnamon, pepper, and salt and cook, stirring constantly, for 30 seconds.

2. Add the chicken, stirring to coat thoroughly, and the tomato sauce. Bring to a boil over medium-high heat, reduce to a simmer, cover, and cook until the chicken is cooked through, about 5 minutes.

3. Stir in the kidney beans and corn and cook, uncovered, until the kidney beans and corn are heated through, about 3 minutes longer. Serve the chili in bowls and top with the sour cream.

Suggested accompaniments: Red-leaf lettuce salad with a Dijon mustard vinaigrette, followed by angel food cake with raspberry sauce.

FAT: 11G/20%
CALORIES: 505
SATURATED FAT: 2.1G
CARBOHYDRATE: 66G
PROTEIN: 41G
CHOLESTEROL: 97MG
SODIUM: 714MG

CHICKEN JAMBALAYA

SERVES: 4
WORKING TIME: 15 MINUTES
TOTAL TIME: 45 MINUTES

Here, traditional Creole ingredients—garlic, onion, tomatoes, and okra—are enhanced by the smoky taste of Canadian bacon.

1 tablespoon olive oil

6 cloves garlic, minced

1 large onion, finely chopped

1 green bell pepper, diced

2 ounces Canadian bacon, coarsely chopped

1 cup reduced-sodium chicken broth, defatted

1⅓ cups long-grain rice

1 cup dry white wine

1 teaspoon dried rosemary

½ teaspoon salt

¼ teaspoon allspice

1 pound skinless, boneless chicken thighs, cut into 1½-inch chunks

1 pound plum tomatoes (about 4), coarsely chopped

10-ounce package frozen whole okra, thawed

1. In a large nonstick skillet, heat the oil until hot but not smoking over medium heat. Add the garlic and onion and cook, stirring occasionally, until the onion has softened, about 5 minutes. Stir in the bell pepper, bacon, and ¼ cup of the broth and cook, stirring occasionally, until the pepper has softened, about 5 minutes.

2. Add the rice, stirring to coat. Add the wine and cook until most of the wine has evaporated, about 5 minutes. Stir in the remaining ¾ cup of broth, the rosemary, salt, allspice, and 1½ cups of water. Bring to a boil over medium-high heat, reduce to a simmer, cover, and cook for 15 minutes.

3. Stir in the chicken, tomatoes, and okra. Return to a boil, reduce to a simmer, cover, and cook until the chicken is cooked through and the rice is tender, about 5 minutes longer. Spoon the jambalaya onto 4 plates and serve.

Suggested accompaniments: Chicory salad with a spicy buttermilk ranch dressing. For dessert, baked honey-glazed bananas.

FAT: 10G/19%
CALORIES: 476
SATURATED FAT: 2.1G
CARBOHYDRATE: 63G
PROTEIN: 33G
CHOLESTEROL: 101MG
SODIUM: 744MG

CHICKEN IN GREEN SAUCE

SERVES: 4
WORKING TIME: 15 MINUTES
TOTAL TIME: 30 MINUTES

1 tablespoon flour

½ teaspoon salt

*¼ teaspoon freshly ground
black pepper*

*4 skinless, boneless chicken
breast halves (about 1 pound
total)*

2 teaspoons olive oil

*1 cup reduced-sodium chicken
broth, defatted*

2 cloves garlic, minced

3 tablespoons fresh lemon juice

*3 tablespoons chopped fresh
parsley*

*2 tablespoons minced chives or
scallion*

½ teaspoon dried tarragon

⅛ teaspoon red pepper flakes

1 cup frozen peas

1. On a plate, combine the flour, ¼ teaspoon of the salt, and the black pepper. Dredge the chicken in the flour mixture, shaking off the excess. In a large nonstick skillet, heat the oil until hot but not smoking over medium heat. Add the chicken and cook until golden brown, turning once, about 5 minutes.

2. Add the broth, garlic, lemon juice, parsley, chives, tarragon, red pepper flakes, and remaining ¼ teaspoon salt. Bring to a boil, reduce to a simmer, and cook, partially covered, until the chicken is cooked through, about 10 minutes longer.

3. With a slotted spoon, transfer the chicken to 4 serving plates. Bring the sauce to a boil over medium-high heat, add the peas, and cook, uncovered, until the sauce is reduced to ½ cup, about 3 minutes. Spoon the peas and sauce over the chicken and serve.

Suggested accompaniments: Roasted red potatoes, and a fresh fruit salad made with watermelon, cantaloupe, and seedless grapes.

FAT: 4G/19%
CALORIES: 193
SATURATED FAT: .7G
CARBOHYDRATE: 9G
PROTEIN: 29G
CHOLESTEROL: 66MG
SODIUM: 550MG

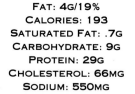

This juicy chicken is bathed in a translucent sauce flecked with herbs and peas, all seasoned with hot red pepper flakes.

CHICKEN GOULASH WITH EGG NOODLES

SERVES: 4
WORKING TIME: 20 MINUTES
TOTAL TIME: 30 MINUTES

12-ounce jar roasted red peppers or pimientos, rinsed and drained

2 tablespoons no-salt-added tomato paste

1 tablespoon mild paprika

1½ teaspoons olive oil

2 medium onions, chopped

4 cloves garlic, minced

2 green bell peppers, diced

3 tablespoons chopped fresh dill, or ¾ teaspoon dried

1¼ cups reduced-sodium chicken broth, defatted

½ teaspoon salt

1 pound skinless, boneless chicken breasts, cut into 2-inch chunks

8 ounces wide egg noodles

⅓ cup plain nonfat yogurt

2 tablespoons flour

3 tablespoons light sour cream

1. In a blender or food processor, combine the roasted peppers, tomato paste, and paprika and purée until smooth. Set aside.

2. In a large nonstick skillet, heat the oil until hot but not smoking over medium heat. Add the onions and garlic and cook, stirring frequently, until the onions are lightly golden, about 4 minutes. Add the peppers and dill and cook for 3 minutes. Stir in the pepper purée, broth, and salt and cook for 1 minute. Add the chicken, bring to a boil, reduce to a simmer, cover, and cook until the chicken is cooked through, about 5 minutes.

3. Meanwhile, in a large pot of boiling water, cook the noodles until just tender. Drain well.

4. In a small bowl, combine the yogurt and flour, stir into the chicken mixture, and cook, uncovered, until the sauce is just thickened, about 3 minutes longer. Place the noodles on 4 plates, spoon the chicken goulash on top, and serve with a dollop of the sour cream.

Suggested accompaniments: Crusty peasant bread, followed by a warm cherry crisp topped with toasted oats for dessert.

FAT: 8G/15%
CALORIES: 485
SATURATED FAT: 2G
CARBOHYDRATE: 63G
PROTEIN: 40G
CHOLESTEROL: 124MG
SODIUM: 595MG

*W*e've flavored this version of the Hungarian specialty with a piquant blend of paprika, tomato paste, and roasted red peppers. Nonfat yogurt adds a creamy texture to the stew. We've mixed it with flour to both thicken the sauce and to stabilize the yogurt so it won't separate during cooking. Light sour cream tops it off.

CHICKEN WITH TOMATOES AND CHICK-PEAS

SERVES: 4
WORKING TIME: 20 MINUTES
TOTAL TIME: 35 MINUTES

The mellow sweetness of honey both tames and beautifully complements the tang of tomatoes in this recipe, while the chick-peas and dried apricots add a delicious, exotic Middle Eastern flair. Chopping the apricots will be easier if you briefly freeze the fruit beforehand.

1 teaspoon olive oil
¾ teaspoon ground cumin
½ teaspoon ground coriander
⅛ teaspoon cayenne pepper
4 bone-in chicken thighs (about 1¼ pounds total), skinned
14½-ounce can no-salt-added stewed tomatoes
2 tablespoons honey
½ teaspoon salt
1 cup orzo or other small pasta
1 cup canned chick-peas, rinsed and drained
¼ cup chopped dried apricots
2 tablespoons chopped fresh parsley

1. In a large nonstick skillet, heat the oil until hot but not smoking over medium heat. Add the cumin, coriander, and cayenne and cook, stirring constantly, for 1 minute. Add the chicken and cook until the chicken is golden brown on all sides, about 5 minutes.

2. Stir in the tomatoes, breaking them up with the back of a spoon. Add the honey and salt, bring to a boil, reduce to a simmer, and cover. Cook until the chicken is cooked through, about 10 minutes longer.

3. Meanwhile, in a large pot of boiling water, cook the orzo until just tender. Drain well.

4. Stir the chick-peas into the chicken mixture and cook, uncovered, until the chick-peas are just heated through, about 2 minutes. Stir in the dried apricots and parsley. Spoon the chicken mixture onto 4 plates, place the orzo on the side, and serve.

Suggested accompaniments: Belgian endive or arugula salad. Follow with vanilla ice milk splashed with coffee liqueur.

FAT: 6G/13%
CALORIES: 422
SATURATED FAT: 1.1G
CARBOHYDRATE: 65G
PROTEIN: 26G
CHOLESTEROL: 67MG
SODIUM: 448MG

This stew is the perfect restorative for a chilly winter evening, with chunks of chicken and colorful vegetables mingling in a creamy sauce. Meltingly tender buttermilk dumplings nestle in the bowl, soaking up all the hearty goodness. Using buttermilk in the dumplings keeps them on the low-fat side.

Parslied Chicken and Dumplings

Serves: 4
Working time: 20 minutes
Total time: 40 minutes

1 cup plus 1 tablespoon flour

½ teaspoon salt

¼ teaspoon freshly ground black pepper

½ pound skinless, boneless chicken thighs, cut into 1½-inch pieces

½ pound skinless, boneless chicken breasts, cut into 1½-inch pieces

2 teaspoons vegetable oil

4 scallions, minced

3 cloves garlic, minced

1 large onion, chopped

1 carrot, diced

½ cup frozen pearl onions, thawed

1 cup reduced-sodium chicken broth, defatted

2 tablespoons chopped fresh parsley

½ teaspoon dried sage

1½ teaspoons baking powder

¼ teaspoon baking soda

⅔ cup low-fat buttermilk

1. On a plate, combine 1 tablespoon of the flour, ¼ teaspoon of the salt, and the pepper. Dredge the chicken in the flour mixture, shaking off the excess. In a large nonstick skillet, heat the oil until hot but not smoking over medium heat. Add the chicken and cook, stirring frequently, until golden brown, about 5 minutes. Transfer the chicken to a plate.

2. Add the scallions, garlic, onion, carrot, and pearl onions to the pan and cook, stirring frequently, until the vegetables begin to soften, about 5 minutes. Stir in the broth, ½ cup of water, the parsley, and sage. Return the chicken to the pan and bring to a boil.

3. Meanwhile, in a medium bowl, combine the remaining 1 cup flour, baking powder, baking soda, and remaining ¼ teaspoon salt. Add the buttermilk and stir to just combine. Drop the mixture by tablespoonfuls onto the boiling chicken mixture to make 8 dumplings (see tip). Cover, reduce to a simmer, and cook until the chicken and dumplings are cooked through, about 10 minutes longer. Spoon the chicken mixture and the dumplings into 4 bowls and serve.

Suggested accompaniments: French bread and a green salad with mushrooms and a white wine vinaigrette. To finish, baked apples sprinkled with cinnamon sugar.

Fat: 6g/16%
Calories: 335
Saturated Fat: 1.3g
Carbohydrate: 38g
Protein: 31g
Cholesterol: 82mg
Sodium: 836mg

TIP

Drop the dumpling mixture onto the boiling chicken mixture, spacing the dumplings about 1 inch apart. For the lightest dumplings, do not uncover the skillet until the full cooking time has elapsed. Dumplings are done when they feel just firm to the touch.

PORT-BRAISED CHICKEN WITH CARROTS AND PARSNIPS

SERVES: 4
WORKING TIME: 20 MINUTES
TOTAL TIME: 45 MINUTES

Port, the renowned brandy-fortified wine traditionally made from Portuguese grapes, creates a deeply flavored sauce for these chicken drumsticks. Parsnips add a delicious nuttiness to the dish but you may use all carrots if preferred. For an easy meal, put brown rice on to steam before you start the chicken.

1 large red onion, cut into 1-inch chunks

4 cloves garlic, minced

2¼ teaspoons sugar

2½ cups reduced-sodium chicken broth, defatted

2 carrots, cut into 1-inch pieces

2 parsnips, cut into 1-inch pieces (about 1½ cups)

½ cup ruby port

3 tablespoons no-salt-added tomato paste

2 tablespoons fresh lemon juice

1 tablespoon Dijon mustard

8 chicken drumsticks (about 2 pounds total), skinned

¼ cup chopped fresh parsley

1. In a nonstick Dutch oven, combine the onion, garlic, sugar, and ½ cup of the broth. Cover and cook over medium heat, stirring occasionally, until the onion has wilted, about 8 minutes.

2. Add the carrots and parsnips, stirring to coat. Stir in the port, tomato paste, lemon juice, mustard, and remaining 2 cups broth and bring to a boil. Add the chicken, reduce to a simmer, cover, and cook, turning the chicken occasionally, until the chicken is cooked through and the vegetables are tender, 15 to 20 minutes.

3. With a slotted spoon, transfer the chicken and vegetables to 4 serving plates. Stir the parsley into the sauce, spoon over the chicken, and serve.

Suggested accompaniments: Steamed brown rice with parsley and grated lemon zest. Follow with broiled pineapple wedges sprinkled with shredded coconut.

FAT: 6G/19%
CALORIES: 281
SATURATED FAT: 1.1G
CARBOHYDRATE: 29G
PROTEIN: 29G
CHOLESTEROL: 94MG
SODIUM: 656MG

CHICKEN PICANTE

SERVES: 4
WORKING TIME: 15 MINUTES
TOTAL TIME: 30 MINUTES

1 tablespoon flour

½ teaspoon salt

¼ teaspoon freshly ground
black pepper

4 skinless, boneless chicken
breast halves (about 1 pound
total)

2 teaspoons olive oil

¾ pound small red potatoes,
diced

¾ cup minced scallions

1 cup reduced-sodium chicken
broth, defatted

¼ cup thinly sliced gherkins

3 tablespoons low-sodium
ketchup

1 tablespoon Dijon mustard

3 tablespoons chopped fresh
parsley

2 tablespoons red wine vinegar

1. On a plate, combine the flour, ¼ teaspoon of the salt, and the pepper. Dredge the chicken in the flour mixture, shaking off the excess. In a large nonstick skillet, heat the oil until hot but not smoking over medium heat. Add the chicken and cook, turning once, until golden brown, about 5 minutes. Transfer the chicken to a plate.

2. Add the potatoes, scallions, ⅓ cup of water, and the remaining ¼ teaspoon salt to the pan. Bring to a boil over medium-high heat, reduce to a simmer, cover, and cook, stirring occasionally, until the potatoes begin to soften, about 6 minutes.

3. Stir in the broth, gherkins, ketchup, and mustard, return to a boil, and cook, uncovered, for 1 minute. Return the chicken to the pan, reduce to a simmer, cover, and cook until the chicken is cooked through, about 8 minutes longer. Stir in the parsley and vinegar. Spoon the chicken mixture onto 4 plates and serve.

Suggested accompaniments: Steamed green beans splashed with red wine vinegar. For dessert, hollowed-out orange shells filled with orange sherbet.

FAT: 4G/14%
CALORIES: 266
SATURATED FAT: .7G
CARBOHYDRATE: 26G
PROTEIN: 29G
CHOLESTEROL: 66MG
SODIUM: 822MG

The richness of the sauce is tartly accented with red wine vinegar and gherkins. As an added bonus, this recipe can be prepared ahead. Refrigerate for up to two days, and then gently reheat on top of the stove or in the microwave at half power. When sautéing chicken, use tongs or a wide spatula for turning—never a fork, which could pierce the meat and release the juices.

CHICKEN FRICASSEE WITH LEEKS AND PEAS

SERVES: 4
WORKING TIME: 25 MINUTES
TOTAL TIME: 35 MINUTES

A creamy sauce enhanced with sage and thyme smoothly coats the chicken and green vegetables. For special dinner guests, garnish the plates with sprigs of fresh herbs. The key to the reduced-fat sauce is evaporated skimmed milk, which is as thick as heavy cream but contributes a fraction of the fat.

2 teaspoons vegetable oil
8 skinless, boneless chicken thighs (about 2 pounds total)
4 leeks, cut into 1-inch pieces
1⅓ cups diced celery
¼ cup flour
2 cups evaporated skimmed milk
1½ cups reduced-sodium chicken broth, defatted
1 teaspoon dried sage
1 teaspoon dried thyme
¼ teaspoon salt
¼ teaspoon freshly ground black pepper
2 cups frozen peas
¼ cup chopped fresh parsley

1. In a nonstick Dutch oven, heat the oil until hot but not smoking over medium heat. Add the chicken and cook until golden brown on all sides, about 5 minutes. Transfer the chicken to a plate.

2. Add the leeks and celery to the pan and cook, stirring frequently, until the vegetables are almost tender, about 5 minutes. Stir in the flour and cook, stirring constantly, until the flour begins to color, about 3 minutes.

3. Gradually stir in the evaporated milk. Add the broth, sage, thyme, salt, and pepper and bring to a boil. Return the chicken to the pan, reduce to a simmer, cover, and cook until the chicken is cooked through and the sauce is slightly thickened, about 10 minutes.

4. Stir in the peas and parsley and cook until the peas are heated through, about 3 minutes longer. Spoon the chicken fricassee onto 4 plates and serve.

Suggested accompaniments: Crusty baguette, and an apple-and-blackberry cobbler afterward.

FAT: 12G/21%
CALORIES: 523
SATURATED FAT: 2.8G
CARBOHYDRATE: 40G
PROTEIN: 61G
CHOLESTEROL: 194MG
SODIUM: 828MG

Arroz con Pollo

SERVES: 4
WORKING TIME: 20 MINUTES
TOTAL TIME: 45 MINUTES

*T*his sunny Spanish dish is a colorful medley, its vivid yellow rice dotted with bell peppers, peas, and bits of smoky Canadian bacon.

1½ teaspoons olive oil

2 ounces Canadian bacon, diced

2 large onions, chopped

4 cloves garlic, minced

2 green bell peppers, diced

2 red bell peppers, diced

2 teaspoons turmeric

1½ pounds skinless, boneless chicken thighs, cut into 1½-inch pieces

1 teaspoon dried oregano

½ teaspoon salt

½ teaspoon freshly ground black pepper

¼ teaspoon cayenne pepper

1½ cups long-grain rice

1⅓ cups frozen peas

1. In a large saucepan, heat the oil until hot but not smoking over medium heat. Add the bacon and onions and cook, stirring frequently, until the onions begin to soften, about 5 minutes. Stir in the garlic, bell peppers, and turmeric and cook for 5 minutes. Add the chicken and cook, stirring frequently, until the chicken is lightly browned, about 5 minutes.

2. Stir in the oregano, salt, black pepper, cayenne pepper, and 5 cups of water and bring to a boil. Add the rice, reduce to a simmer, cover, and cook until the rice is tender and the chicken is cooked through, about 17 minutes.

3. Stir in the peas and cook, uncovered, until the peas are heated through, about 3 minutes longer. Spoon the chicken and rice mixture onto 4 plates and serve.

Suggested accompaniment: Broiled peach halves sprinkled with crumbled amaretti cookies for dessert.

FAT: 10G/15%
CALORIES: 593
SATURATED FAT: 2.4G
CARBOHYDRATE: 77G
PROTEIN: 46G
CHOLESTEROL: 148MG
SODIUM: 682MG

BAKED & ROASTED

3

CHILI-"FRIED" CHICKEN WITH RICE PILAF

SERVES: 4
WORKING TIME: 15 MINUTES
TOTAL TIME: 30 MINUTES

Even though this deliciously crisp, chili-cornmeal-coated chicken seems fried, it's actually oven-baked, eliminating the extra oil for frying. For moistness and an added tanginess, we've briefly marinated the chicken in buttermilk, a natural tenderizer. If buttermilk is not on hand, just combine one cup low-fat milk with one tablespoon lemon juice. Let stand for five minutes to sour.

1 cup long-grain rice
½ teaspoon salt
½ cup finely chopped carrot
¼ cup finely chopped green bell pepper
¼ cup finely chopped onion
4 skinless, boneless chicken breast halves (about 1 pound total)
1 cup low-fat buttermilk
½ cup flour
2 tablespoons yellow cornmeal
2 teaspoons mild chili powder
½ teaspoon dried oregano
⅛ teaspoon cayenne pepper
2 teaspoons vegetable oil
1 tablespoon chopped fresh parsley

1. In a medium saucepan, combine the rice, 2 cups of water, and ¼ teaspoon of the salt. Bring to a boil over high heat, reduce to a simmer, cover, and cook for 10 minutes. Stir in the carrot, bell pepper, and onion, cover, and cook until the rice is tender, about 7 minutes longer.

2. Meanwhile, preheat the oven to 400°. Spray a baking sheet with nonstick cooking spray. In a shallow bowl, combine the chicken and buttermilk and let stand for 5 minutes.

3. On a plate, combine the flour, cornmeal, chili powder, oregano, remaining ¼ teaspoon salt, and the cayenne pepper. Dredge the chicken in the flour mixture, shaking off the excess. Place the chicken on the prepared baking sheet, drizzle with the oil, and bake for 12 minutes, or until the chicken is crisp, golden, and cooked through.

4. Stir the parsley into the rice pilaf and spoon onto 4 plates. Place the chicken on a cutting board and cut the chicken into diagonal slices. Arrange the chicken on the plates with the pilaf and serve.

Suggested accompaniments: Sautéed green beans and yellow squash sprinkled with sliced almonds. For dessert, vanilla ice milk topped with diced mango.

FAT: 5G/10%
CALORIES: 429
SATURATED FAT: 1.1G
CARBOHYDRATE: 59G
PROTEIN: 34G
CHOLESTEROL: 68MG
SODIUM: 431MG

HERBED CHICKEN WITH ORZO AND SPINACH

SERVES: 4
WORKING TIME: 15 MINUTES
TOTAL TIME: 35 MINUTES

2 tablespoons fresh lemon juice

¾ teaspoon dried rosemary

¾ teaspoon dried oregano

½ teaspoon sweet paprika

½ teaspoon salt

4 bone-in chicken breast halves (about 1½ pounds total), with skin

1 cup orzo

2 teaspoons olive oil

2 cloves garlic, minced

10-ounce package frozen chopped spinach, thawed and squeezed dry

¼ teaspoon sugar

⅛ teaspoon ground nutmeg

3 tablespoons dried currants or dark raisins

2 teaspoons pine nuts

1. Preheat the oven to 400°. In a small bowl, combine 4 teaspoons of the lemon juice, ½ teaspoon of the rosemary, ½ teaspoon of the oregano, the paprika, and ¼ teaspoon of the salt. With your fingers, carefully separate the skin from the chicken, leaving the skin intact. Spread the lemon-herb mixture under the skin, rubbing it into the meat. Place the chicken on a rack in a medium baking pan and bake for 20 minutes, or until the chicken is cooked through.

2. Meanwhile, in a large pot of boiling water, cook the orzo until just tender. Drain and set aside.

3. In a large nonstick skillet, heat the oil until hot but not smoking over medium heat. Add the garlic and cook, stirring frequently, for 30 seconds. Stir in the spinach, sugar, nutmeg, remaining ¼ teaspoon rosemary, remaining ¼ teaspoon oregano, and remaining ¼ teaspoon salt and cook until the spinach is heated through, about 5 minutes. Stir in the orzo, currants, pine nuts, and remaining 2 teaspoons lemon juice and cook until the orzo is heated through, about 2 minutes longer.

4. Place the chicken and the orzo-spinach mixture on 4 plates. Remove the skin from the chicken and serve.

Suggested accompaniments: Thin bread sticks, and fresh orange wedges.

FAT: 10G/22%
CALORIES: 410
SATURATED FAT: 2.2G
CARBOHYDRATE: 47G
PROTEIN: 33G
CHOLESTEROL: 72MG
SODIUM: 400MG

Rubbing rosemary, oregano, and paprika beneath the skin infuses this chicken with a wonderful flavor. The fat stays in the skin, which is removed before serving, and the herbs stay on the chicken itself. The orzo, a rice-shaped pasta, has a creamy texture that creates the feeling of added richness in this fit-for-company dinner.

We've sensibly updated this time-honored favorite without sacrificing any of its soothing comfort-food qualities. Crisp, golden phyllo is a delicious alternative to the fat-laden crust found in a more traditional pot pie. The filling, thick with vegetables and tender pieces of chicken, is creamy but deceptively so—the secret is evaporated skimmed milk.

CHICKEN POT PIE

SERVES: 4
WORKING TIME: 25 MINUTES
TOTAL TIME: 50 MINUTES

1 cup reduced-sodium chicken broth, defatted

3 carrots, cut into ½-inch chunks

1 all-purpose potato, peeled and cut into ½-inch chunks

1 parsnip, cut into ½-inch chunks

½ teaspoon salt

1 cup frozen pearl onions

1 cup frozen peas

1 pound skinless, boneless chicken thighs, cut into 2-inch pieces

½ cup evaporated skimmed milk

¼ cup flour

½ teaspoon dried sage

¼ teaspoon freshly ground black pepper

Two 17 x 11-inch sheets phyllo dough, cut crosswise in half

1. Preheat the oven to 375°. In a large saucepan, combine the broth, carrots, potato, parsnip, and ¼ teaspoon of the salt. Bring to a boil over high heat, reduce to a simmer, and cover. Cook until the potato is almost tender, about 5 minutes. Stir in the pearl onions, peas, and chicken, return to a boil, reduce to a simmer, and cover. Cook until the chicken is cooked through, about 5 minutes.

2. Meanwhile, in a small saucepan, combine the evaporated milk, flour, sage, pepper, and remaining ¼ teaspoon salt and stir to blend. Bring to a boil, reduce to a simmer, and cook until the sauce has thickened to the consistency of heavy cream, about 2 minutes. Stir in the chicken mixture and cook for 1 minute longer.

3. Mound the chicken mixture into a 9-inch deep-dish pie pan. Layer the phyllo sheets on top, overlapping the sheets at right angles (see tip; top photo), tucking in the edges (middle photo), and lightly spraying each sheet with nonstick cooking spray. Using a small, sharp knife, cut a 3-inch X in the center of the pie, pull back the corners (bottom photo), and lightly spray the corners with nonstick cooking spray. Bake the pot pie for 15 minutes, or until the filling is heated through and the phyllo is crisp and lightly golden.

Suggested accompaniments: Watercress and endive salad with a citrus vinaigrette and, for dessert, a reduced-fat chocolate pudding made with ground cinnamon.

FAT: 6G/16%
CALORIES: 337
SATURATED FAT: 1.3G
CARBOHYDRATE: 40G
PROTEIN: 31G
CHOLESTEROL: 95MG
SODIUM: 682MG

TIP

Roast Chicken with Pecan-Rice Dressing

SERVES: 4
WORKING TIME: 30 MINUTES
TOTAL TIME: 1 HOUR 20 MINUTES

This chicken is perfumed with a shallot-garlic mixture spread under the skin, and is further complemented by a savory mushroom, rice, and pecan dressing, baked separately. The secret to moist white meat is roasting the chicken breast-side down for the first half of cooking, and then turning the bird breast-side up for the remaining time and basting occasionally.

3 shallots or scallions, minced
¼ cup chopped fresh basil
3 cloves garlic, minced
1 teaspoon olive oil
¾ teaspoon salt
¼ teaspoon dried sage
3½-pound whole chicken
2 tablespoons fresh lemon juice
1 large onion, diced
1 carrot, finely chopped
2 cups thinly sliced mushrooms
1 cup long-grain rice
4 teaspoons chopped pecans
2 cups reduced-sodium chicken broth, defatted
¼ cup flour

1. Preheat the oven to 375°. In a small bowl, combine the shallots, 2 tablespoons of the basil, one-third of the garlic, oil, ½ teaspoon of the salt, and sage. Sprinkle the chicken cavity with the lemon juice. With your fingers, carefully loosen the skin from the breast, leaving the skin intact. Spread the shallot mixture under the skin. Truss the chicken by tying together the legs with string. Place the chicken, breast-side down, on a rack in a small roasting pan and roast for 30 minutes. Turn the chicken breast-side up, and continue to roast, basting occasionally with the pan juices, for 30 minutes longer, or until the chicken is cooked through.

2. Meanwhile, in a medium flameproof casserole, combine the onion, carrot, remaining garlic, and ¼ cup of water. Cook over medium heat for 5 minutes. Add the mushrooms. Cook for 5 minutes. Stir in the rice, pecans, 1¾ cups of water, the remaining 2 tablespoons basil, and remaining ¼ teaspoon salt. Cover, place in the oven with the chicken, and bake for 30 minutes, or until the rice is tender.

3. Place the chicken on a platter and pour off the fat from the pan. Add the broth to the pan and bring to a boil, stirring to loosen the browned bits. Whisk in the flour until smooth and cook, whisking, until thickened, 3 to 5 minutes. Serve the chicken with the dressing and gravy. Remove the skin from the chicken before eating.

Suggested accompaniments: Sautéed greens and cherry tomatoes.

FAT: 14G/23%
CALORIES: 550
SATURATED FAT: 3.3G
CARBOHYDRATE: 54G
PROTEIN: 50G
CHOLESTEROL: 127MG
SODIUM: 866MG

For
these rosemary- and oregano-scented chicken burgers, tenderized and moistened with nonfat yogurt, we first sear the patties quickly in a nonstick skillet, and then finish them in the oven to retain the juices. The crispy baked sweet potato chips are a delectable stand-in for fries. And the cranberry-apricot sauce is a perfect accent for the burgers.

CHICKEN BURGERS WITH SWEET POTATO CHIPS

SERVES: 4
WORKING TIME: 20 MINUTES
TOTAL TIME: 1 HOUR 10 MINUTES

¾ pound sweet potatoes, peeled and cut into ⅛-inch-thick slices

1 pound skinless, boneless chicken thighs, cut into small pieces

⅓ cup finely chopped scallions

¼ cup plain nonfat yogurt

¼ cup dried bread crumbs

1 tablespoon Dijon mustard

½ teaspoon dried rosemary

½ teaspoon dried oregano

½ teaspoon salt

2 teaspoons vegetable oil

1 cup cranberry sauce (not jellied)

3 tablespoons apricot jam

1. In a medium bowl, combine the sweet potatoes with cold water to cover and let stand for 30 minutes. Preheat the oven to 400°. Spray 2 baking sheets with nonstick cooking spray. Drain the sweet potatoes and pat dry. Arrange the sweet potatoes in a single layer on the prepared baking sheets and bake for 20 to 25 minutes, or until the potato chips are crisp.

2. Meanwhile, in a food processor, process the chicken until a coarse paste forms. In a medium bowl, combine the ground chicken, scallions, yogurt, bread crumbs, 2 teaspoons of the mustard, rosemary, oregano, and salt and mix gently to just blend. Shape the mixture into 4 patties (see tip).

3. In a large nonstick ovenproof skillet, heat the oil until hot but not smoking over medium heat. Add the patties and cook until browned, about 2 minutes per side. Remove the sweet potato chips from the oven and set aside. Place the skillet in the oven and bake for 10 minutes, or until the burgers are cooked through.

4. In a small bowl, combine the cranberry sauce, jam, and remaining 1 teaspoon mustard and stir to blend. Place the burgers, sweet potato chips, and sauce on 4 plates and serve.

Suggested accompaniments: Lettuce and tomato slices with an herb vinaigrette. To finish, strawberries with reduced-fat fudge sauce for dipping.

FAT: 8G/18%
CALORIES: 409
SATURATED FAT: 1.6G
CARBOHYDRATE: 59G
PROTEIN: 26G
CHOLESTEROL: 94MG
SODIUM: 525MG

TIP

With moistened hands (this prevents sticking), shape the chicken mixture into four patties, each about ½ inch thick. Shape the patties gently—overhandling makes the burgers more compact, which toughens them.

GLAZED HONEY-MUSTARD CHICKEN

SERVES 4
WORKING TIME: 15 MINUTES
TOTAL TIME: 35 MINUTES

A

savory honey-mustard mixture is the basis for both the under-the-skin shallot stuffing, and the rich lemony sauce in this recipe.

3 tablespoons Dijon mustard

2 tablespoons plus 1 teaspoon honey

¼ teaspoon salt

1 tablespoon minced shallot or onion

1 tablespoon chopped fresh parsley

½ teaspoon dried sage

3 tablespoons fresh lemon juice

4 bone-in chicken breast halves (about 1½ pounds total), with skin

1 tablespoon minced scallion

1. Preheat the oven to 400°. In a small bowl, combine the mustard, honey, and salt and stir to blend. In a cup, combine the shallot, parsley, sage, 2 tablespoons of the honey-mustard mixture, and 1 tablespoon of the lemon juice. Reserve the remaining honey-mustard mixture.

2. With your fingers, carefully separate the skin from the chicken, leaving the skin intact. Spread the shallot-mustard mixture under the skin, rubbing it into the meat. Place the chicken on a rack in a medium baking pan and bake for 20 minutes, or until the chicken is cooked through.

3. Add the remaining 2 tablespoons lemon juice and the scallion to the reserved honey-mustard mixture and stir to blend. Place the chicken on 4 plates and remove the skin. Skim the fat from the pan juices and stir the juices into the scallion-mustard mixture. Spoon the sauce over the chicken and serve.

Suggested accompaniments: Steamed green beans and julienned carrots. For dessert, broiled plum halves with a dollop of sweetened light sour cream.

FAT: 4G/19%
CALORIES: 186
SATURATED FAT: .8G
CARBOHYDRATE: 12G
PROTEIN: 25G
CHOLESTEROL: 68MG
SODIUM: 536MG

CHICKEN PARMESAN WITH HERBED TOMATOES

SERVES: 4
WORKING TIME: 10 MINUTES
TOTAL TIME: 30 MINUTES

2 egg whites
⅓ cup dried bread crumbs
¼ cup grated Parmesan cheese
¼ teaspoon salt
4 skinless, boneless chicken breast halves (about 1 pound total)
2 teaspoons olive oil
2 tomatoes, cut into 12 slices
¾ teaspoon sugar
¾ teaspoon dried oregano
¼ teaspoon dried marjoram

1. Preheat the oven to 400°. Spray a baking sheet with nonstick cooking spray.

2. In a shallow dish, using a fork, beat the egg whites and 1 tablespoon water until foamy. On a plate, combine the bread crumbs, Parmesan, and salt. Set aside 2 tablespoons of the crumb mixture. Dip the chicken into the egg whites, then into the crumb mixture, gently pressing crumbs into the chicken. Place the chicken on the prepared baking sheet, drizzle with the oil, and bake for 12 minutes, or until the chicken is crisp, golden, and cooked through.

3. Meanwhile, arrange the tomatoes in a single layer on another baking sheet and sprinkle with the sugar, oregano, and marjoram. Spoon the reserved 2 tablespoons crumb mixture on top, gently pressing crumbs into the tomatoes. Place the tomatoes in the oven with the chicken and bake for 6 to 8 minutes, or until the tomatoes are heated through and the topping is crisp. Place the chicken and tomatoes on 4 plates and serve.

Suggested accompaniments: Roasted zucchini chunks, followed by toasted slices of reduced-fat pound cake topped with fresh blueberries.

FAT: 6G/23%
CALORIES: 230
SATURATED FAT: 1.8G
CARBOHYDRATE: 11G
PROTEIN: 32G
CHOLESTEROL: 70MG
SODIUM: 412MG

Cheese is not off limits in this Italian-inspired entrée—aromatic Parmesan adds just the right flavor.

BUFFALO CHICKEN STRIPS

SERVES: 4
WORKING TIME: 15 MINUTES
TOTAL TIME: 25 MINUTES

½ cup low-fat (1%) milk

½ teaspoon honey

1 pound skinless, boneless chicken breasts, cut into 1-inch-wide strips

1 cup crushed cornflakes (about 2 cups uncrushed)

¼ teaspoon ground ginger

¼ teaspoon dried thyme

¼ teaspoon dried rosemary

1 cup plain nonfat yogurt

2 ounces blue cheese, crumbled

½ cup minced scallions

6 drops hot pepper sauce

2 carrots, cut into sticks

2 ribs celery with leaves, cut into sticks

1. Preheat the oven to 400°. Line a baking sheet with foil and spray with nonstick cooking spray. In a shallow bowl, combine the milk and honey and stir to blend. Add the chicken strips, stir to coat, and let stand for 10 minutes.

2. Meanwhile, on a plate, combine the cornflakes, ginger, thyme, and rosemary. Dip the chicken strips into the cornflake mixture to coat thoroughly, gently pressing cornflakes into the chicken. Place the chicken on the prepared baking sheet and bake for 8 minutes, or until the chicken is crisp, golden, and cooked through.

3. In a medium bowl, combine the yogurt, blue cheese, scallions, and hot pepper sauce and stir to blend. Place the chicken and the carrot and celery sticks on 4 plates and serve with the blue cheese dip.

Suggested accompaniments: Iced herbal tea, and a dessert of raspberry sorbet served with miniature nonfat cookies.

For this popular finger food, we've substituted lean chicken breast for the usual wings and then soaked the strips in low-fat milk and honey for extra tenderness. The creamy base for the dip is nonfat yogurt rather than sour cream. To crush cornflakes, place them in a resealable plastic bag, seal, and run a rolling pin or heavy glass over the bag.

FAT: 6G/15%
CALORIES: 357
SATURATED FAT: 3.3G
CARBOHYDRATE: 37G
PROTEIN: 37G
CHOLESTEROL: 79MG
SODIUM: 716MG

Baked Chicken in Parchment

SERVES: 4
WORKING TIME: 15 MINUTES
TOTAL TIME: 40 MINUTES

*T*his chicken, steamed in foil or in parchment (a type of paper treated for cooking), is meltingly tender, with a rich mushroom taste.

½ pound mushrooms, finely chopped

3 cloves garlic, minced

1 carrot, diced

½ cup reduced-sodium chicken broth, defatted

⅓ cup dry red wine

½ teaspoon salt

4 skinless, boneless chicken breast halves (about 1 pound total)

1 tablespoon fresh lemon juice

½ teaspoon dried thyme

4 thin slices smoked turkey (about 2 ounces)

1. Preheat the oven to 425°. Spray four 10-inch sheets of parchment paper or foil with nonstick cooking spray.

2. In a large nonstick skillet, combine the mushrooms, garlic, carrot, and broth. Cook, partially covered, over medium-low heat until the vegetables are tender, about 5 minutes. Add the wine and salt, increase the heat to high, and cook until the liquid has evaporated, about 5 minutes. Remove from the heat.

3. Place 1 chicken breast half on the top half of each parchment sheet, sprinkle with the lemon juice and thyme, and spoon the mushroom mixture on top. Place 1 slice of turkey on top of each chicken breast, fold the parchment over the chicken, and crimp the edges to seal. Place the packets on a baking sheet and bake for 12 to 15 minutes, or until the chicken is cooked through.

4. Place the packets on 4 plates. Cut a cross in the center of each packet, pull back the paper, and serve. Open the packets carefully because the mixture may steam.

Suggested accompaniments: Romaine, red onion, and cherry tomato salad with a reduced-fat garlic dressing. For dessert, fresh pineapple slices brushed with maple syrup and grilled.

FAT: 3G/14%
CALORIES: 191
SATURATED FAT: .6G
CARBOHYDRATE: 6G
PROTEIN: 31G
CHOLESTEROL: 73MG
SODIUM: 581MG

ASIAN CHICKEN ROLL-UPS

SERVES: 4
WORKING TIME: 20 MINUTES
TOTAL TIME: 45 MINUTES

3 strips orange zest, each about 3 inches long

6 tablespoons orange juice

3 tablespoons reduced-sodium soy sauce

3 tablespoons firmly packed dark brown sugar

2 cloves garlic, crushed

1 teaspoon peanut oil

1 pound skinless, boneless chicken thighs

2 plums, pitted and coarsely chopped

1 tablespoon fresh lemon juice

Eight 6-inch flour tortillas

4 scallions, cut into 2-inch julienne strips

1 carrot, cut into 2-inch julienne strips

2 cups alfalfa sprouts

1. In a medium bowl, combine the orange zest, 3 tablespoons of the orange juice, soy sauce, 2 tablespoons of the brown sugar, garlic, and peanut oil. Add the chicken, stirring to coat. Cover and refrigerate for 30 minutes or up to 2 hours.

2. Meanwhile, in a medium saucepan, combine the plums, lemon juice, the remaining 3 tablespoons orange juice, and remaining 1 tablespoon brown sugar. Bring to a boil over medium-high heat, reduce to a simmer, and cook, stirring occasionally, until the plums are tender and the sauce thickens, about 10 minutes.

3. Preheat the oven to 350°. Line a small baking pan with foil. Place the chicken in the prepared pan, reserving ¼ cup of the marinade, and bake, basting occasionally with the reserved marinade, for 15 minutes, or until the chicken is cooked through. Wrap the tortillas in foil and place in the oven with the chicken for 5 minutes, or until the tortillas are heated through.

4. Transfer the chicken to a cutting board. Skim the fat from the pan juices and stir 2 tablespoons of the juices into the plum sauce. Shred the chicken and combine with the scallions and carrot. Place the tortillas on 4 plates and place the chicken mixture, half of the plum sauce, and the sprouts on top. Roll up the tortillas, secure with toothpicks, and serve with the remaining plum sauce.

Suggested accompaniment: Iced lemonade with mint.

FAT: 9G/22%
CALORIES: 373
SATURATED FAT: 1.8G
CARBOHYDRATE: 45G
PROTEIN: 28G
CHOLESTEROL: 94MG
SODIUM: 754MG

Served *with a tart-sweet plum sauce, these hand-held tortilla "sandwiches" make an attractive lunch or light supper.*

CHICKEN AND SWEET POTATOES WITH ROSEMARY

SERVES: 4
WORKING TIME: 15 MINUTES
TOTAL TIME: 50 MINUTES

For this easy-to-prepare entrée, the chicken and sweet potatoes are enhanced with a touch of deeply flavored rosemary-garlic oil and then baked together. Sweet potatoes are at their very best during the late fall and early winter. Select smooth-skinned potatoes with tapered ends and no bruises.

4 bone-in chicken breast halves (about 1½ pounds total), skinned

2 pounds sweet potatoes, peeled and cut into ¼-inch-thick slices

3 cloves garlic, minced

1 tablespoon plus 1 teaspoon olive oil

1½ teaspoons dried rosemary

½ teaspoon freshly ground black pepper

½ teaspoon salt

1 tablespoon fresh lemon juice

1. Preheat the oven to 425°. Spray a large roasting pan with nonstick cooking spray. Place the chicken in the prepared pan. Arrange the sweet potato slices around the chicken, overlapping them slightly. In a cup, combine the garlic, oil, rosemary, pepper, and salt and stir to blend. Spoon the garlic mixture over the chicken and sweet potatoes. Drizzle the chicken with the lemon juice.

2. Bake the chicken and sweet potatoes, turning the sweet potatoes once or twice, for 30 minutes, or until the chicken is cooked through. Transfer the chicken to 4 serving plates and cover with foil to keep warm.

3. Turn up the oven to 500°. Bake the sweet potatoes for 8 to 10 minutes longer, or until the sweet potatoes are tender. Place the sweet potatoes on the plates with the chicken and serve.

Suggested accompaniments: Sugar snap peas tossed with grated orange zest, and a Belgian endive salad with a red wine vinaigrette.

FAT 7G/18%
CALORIES 342
SATURATED FAT 1G
PROTEIN 29G
CARBOHYDRATE 41G
CHOLESTEROL 65MG
SODIUM 368MG

LEMON CHICKEN WITH ROAST POTATOES AND GARLIC

SERVES: 4
WORKING TIME: 20 MINUTES
TOTAL TIME: 1 HOUR 20 MINUTES

This scrumptious recipe could easily become a favorite for Sunday dinner. The whole chicken is scented with lemon and herbs tucked inside the cavity and under the skin. Roasting the chicken on a rack in a pan lets the fat drain away. To prevent the potatoes from absorbing fat from the chicken, they're roasted in a separate pan.

1 pound small red potatoes, cut into quarters

6 cloves garlic, 2 unpeeled and 4 peeled

4 sprigs fresh thyme, or 1 teaspoon dried

2 sprigs fresh rosemary, or ¾ teaspoon dried

¾ teaspoon salt

½ teaspoon freshly ground black pepper

1 teaspoon olive oil

3½-pound whole chicken

1 bay leaf

2 lemons, 1 pierced several times with a fork, the other thinly sliced

1. Preheat the oven to 375°. In a medium baking pan, combine the potatoes, the 2 unpeeled garlic cloves, 2 sprigs of the thyme or ½ teaspoon of the dried, 1 sprig of the rosemary or ½ teaspoon of the dried, ¼ teaspoon of the salt, and ¼ teaspoon of the pepper. Drizzle the potatoes with the oil and toss to combine. Set aside.

2. Sprinkle the chicken cavity with the remaining ½ teaspoon salt and remaining ¼ teaspoon pepper. Place the bay leaf, the 4 peeled cloves garlic, and the pierced lemon in the cavity. With your fingers, carefully loosen the skin from the breast, leaving the skin intact. Tuck the remaining 2 sprigs thyme or ½ teaspoon dried, remaining 1 sprig rosemary or ¼ teaspoon dried, and the lemon slices under the skin. Truss the chicken by tying together the legs with string. Place the chicken, breast-side down, on a rack in a small roasting pan.

3. Place the chicken and potatoes in the oven and roast for 30 minutes. Turn the chicken breast-side up, and continue to roast for 30 minutes longer, basting the chicken with pan juices and stirring the potatoes occasionally, or until the chicken is cooked through and the potatoes are tender. Place the chicken and potatoes on a platter. Remove the skin from the chicken before eating.

Suggested accompaniments: Steamed broccoli with diced red onion, and a fresh fruit bowl of apples, pears, and red and green seedless grapes.

FAT: 12G/28%
CALORIES: 392
SATURATED FAT: 3.1G
CARBOHYDRATE: 28G
PROTEIN: 44G
CHOLESTEROL: 127MG
SODIUM: 546MG

The stuffing for these chicken breasts tastes decadently rich, but the fat content is surprisingly low. The trick is using a blend of reduced-fat cheeses—ricotta and cream cheese—to achieve a silky texture. Thyme-sprinkled potatoes are a wonderfully fragrant accompaniment.

SPINACH-AND-CHEESE-STUFFED CHICKEN

SERVES: 4
WORKING TIME: 15 MINUTES
TOTAL TIME: 45 MINUTES

1 pound all-purpose potatoes, peeled and thinly sliced

¼ teaspoon dried thyme

½ teaspoon salt

⅓ cup reduced-sodium chicken broth, defatted

Half 10-ounce package frozen chopped spinach, thawed and squeezed dry

½ cup part-skim ricotta cheese

2 tablespoons reduced-fat cream cheese

2 tablespoons minced shallot or scallion

1 egg white

1 teaspoon grated lemon zest

⅛ teaspoon freshly ground black pepper

Pinch ground nutmeg

4 bone-in chicken breast halves (about 1½ pounds), with skin

1. Preheat the oven to 400°. In a large saucepan, combine the potatoes with water to cover. Bring to a boil over high heat, reduce to a simmer, cover, and cook for 5 minutes. Drain and pat dry. Spray a medium baking pan with nonstick cooking spray. Add the potatoes, thyme, and ¼ teaspoon of the salt and toss to combine. Pour the broth on top and set aside.

2. In a medium bowl, combine the spinach, ricotta, cream cheese, shallot, egg white, zest, pepper, nutmeg, and the remaining ¼ teaspoon salt and stir to blend. With your fingers, carefully loosen the skin from the chicken, leaving the skin intact (see tip). Spread the spinach mixture under the skin. Place the chicken on a rack in a separate medium baking pan.

3. Place the chicken and potatoes in the oven and bake for 25 minutes, or until the chicken is cooked through and the potatoes are tender. Place the chicken and potatoes on 4 serving plates. Skim the fat from the pan juices, spoon some of the juices on top of the potatoes, and serve. Remove the skin from the chicken before eating.

Suggested accompaniments: Julienned red bell peppers and carrots, and applesauce flavored with ground ginger for dessert.

FAT: 7G/21%
CALORIES: 294
SATURATED FAT: 2.9G
CARBOHYDRATE: 24G
PROTEIN: 34G
CHOLESTEROL: 79MG
SODIUM: 497MG

TIP

Tucking the stuffing beneath the skin is a clever way to have stuffing without roasting a whole bird. Carefully loosen the chicken skin from the flesh from an open side, leaving the skin attached along the other side. Spoon the stuffing under the skin and then press gently down on the skin, spreading the stuffing evenly.

OVEN-BARBECUED CHICKEN BREASTS

SERVES: 4
WORKING TIME: 10 MINUTES
TOTAL TIME: 40 MINUTES

*F*inishing *these tempting chicken breasts with a quick pass under the broiler richly caramelizes the honey- and pineapple-sweetened sauce.*

1 teaspoon olive oil

2 cloves garlic, minced

1 cup no-salt-added canned tomatoes

½ cup pineapple juice

3 tablespoons honey

1 tablespoon cider vinegar

1 tablespoon molasses

¾ teaspoon ground ginger

½ teaspoon salt

4 bone-in chicken breast halves (about 1½ pounds total), skinned

1. Preheat the oven to 425°. In a medium saucepan, heat the oil until hot but not smoking over medium heat. Add the garlic and cook, stirring frequently, until softened, about 30 seconds. Stir in the tomatoes, breaking them up with the back of a spoon. Add the pineapple juice, honey, vinegar, molasses, ginger, and salt, bring to a boil, and cook until the sauce has thickened, about 5 minutes.

2. Spray a shallow medium roasting pan with nonstick cooking spray. Place the chicken in the prepared pan, spoon the sauce on top, and bake for 20 minutes, or until the chicken is cooked through.

3. Preheat the broiler. Broil the chicken 4 inches from the heat for 2 minutes, or until the sauce has caramelized. Place the chicken on 4 plates and serve.

Suggested accompaniments: Dilled corn on the cob and crusty rolls. Follow with lemon frozen yogurt.

FAT: 3G/12%
CALORIES: 226
SATURATED FAT: .5G
CARBOHYDRATE: 24G
PROTEIN: 27G
CHOLESTEROL: 65MG
SODIUM: 357MG

CHICKEN, VEGETABLE, AND CORN BREAD CASSEROLE

SERVES: 4
WORKING TIME: 15 MINUTES
TOTAL TIME: 40 MINUTES

Two 8-ounce cans no-salt-added tomato sauce

1 green bell pepper, diced

1 large onion, diced

2 teaspoons sugar

½ teaspoon dried oregano

1 cup frozen corn kernels

¾ teaspoon salt

1 pound skinless, boneless chicken thighs, cut into 2-inch pieces

⅓ cup yellow cornmeal

⅓ cup flour

½ teaspoon baking powder

¼ teaspoon baking soda

½ cup low-fat buttermilk

1 teaspoon vegetable oil

1 egg white

1. Preheat the oven to 400°. In a medium saucepan, combine the tomato sauce, bell pepper, onion, 1 teaspoon of the sugar, and oregano. Bring to a boil over medium-high heat, reduce to a simmer, and cook, stirring occasionally, until the vegetables begin to soften, about 5 minutes. Stir in the corn and ½ teaspoon of the salt. Return to a boil, add the chicken, and cook for 1 minute. Spoon the chicken mixture into a 9-inch pie pan.

2. In a medium bowl, combine the cornmeal, flour, baking powder, baking soda, the remaining 1 teaspoon sugar, and the remaining ¼ teaspoon salt. Stir in the buttermilk, oil, and egg white until just combined. Spoon the cornmeal mixture onto the center of the chicken mixture. Place the pie pan on a baking sheet and bake the casserole for 20 to 25 minutes, or until the chicken is cooked through and the corn bread is golden brown.

Suggested accompaniment: Stewed rhubarb and strawberry compote for dessert.

FAT: 7G/18%
CALORIES: 347
SATURATED FAT: 1.5G
CARBOHYDRATE: 42G
PROTEIN: 30G
CHOLESTEROL: 95MG
SODIUM: 721MG

The golden corn bread "crust" gives this easy chicken and vegetable combination extra appeal.

BAKED CHICKEN WITH CITRUS SAUCE

SERVES: 4
WORKING TIME: 20 MINUTES
TOTAL TIME: 50 MINUTES

This dish sings with the fresh taste of lemon and oranges. Using cornstarch instead of flour as a thickener makes a clear rather than an opaque sauce, and eliminates the risk of a raw flour taste. To prevent lumping, mix cornstarch in a little cold liquid before adding it to a hot mixture. Do not cook the sauce too long or the cornstarch will lose its thickening power.

2 teaspoons olive oil

3 cloves garlic, minced

1 tablespoon minced chives or scallion tops

½ cup orange juice

2 tablespoons fresh lemon juice

⅔ cup reduced-sodium chicken broth, defatted

4 bone-in chicken breast halves (about 1½ pounds total), with skin

½ teaspoon salt

2 thin navel orange slices, each cut in half

2 thin lemon slices, each cut in half

2 teaspoons cornstarch

2 tablespoons chopped fresh parsley

1. Preheat the oven to 400°. In a small nonstick skillet, heat the oil until hot but not smoking over medium heat. Add the garlic and chives and cook, stirring frequently, for 3 minutes. Add the orange juice and lemon juice. Increase the heat to medium-high, bring to a boil, and cook for 2 minutes. Add the broth and cook until the flavors are blended, about 1 minute longer. Remove from the heat.

2. With your fingers, carefully loosen the skin from the chicken, leaving the skin intact. Rub the salt over the meat, then tuck an orange slice and a lemon slice under the skin of each chicken breast. Place the chicken on a rack in a medium roasting pan, pour the orange juice mixture on top, and bake for 20 to 25 minutes, or until the chicken is cooked through.

3. Place the chicken on 4 serving plates and remove the skin and fruit slices. Skim the fat from the pan juices and bring to a boil over medium-high heat. In a cup, combine the cornstarch and 1 tablespoon water, stir to blend, and stir into the boiling juices. Cook, stirring constantly, until the sauce is slightly thickened, about 3 minutes. Stir in the parsley, spoon the sauce over the chicken, and serve.

Suggested accompaniments: Green peas with pearl onions and steamed red potatoes. For dessert, pears poached in cranberry juice.

FAT: 5G/23%
CALORIES: 194
SATURATED FAT: 1.1G
CARBOHYDRATE: 11G
PROTEIN: 26G
CHOLESTEROL: 68MG
SODIUM: 443MG

CRISPY CHICKEN WITH CORN CHOWCHOW

SERVES: 4
WORKING TIME: 20 MINUTES
TOTAL TIME: 45 MINUTES

4 whole chicken legs (about 2 pounds total), skinned
⅔ cup low-fat buttermilk
¼ cup red wine vinegar
3 tablespoons sugar
1 cup frozen corn kernels
1 red bell pepper, diced
1 green bell pepper, diced
6 scallions, finely chopped
2 tablespoons chopped fresh parsley
¾ teaspoon salt
⅓ cup yellow cornmeal
⅓ cup flour
¼ cup dried bread crumbs

1. Preheat the oven to 400°. Spray a baking sheet with nonstick cooking spray. In a shallow bowl, combine the chicken and buttermilk and let stand for 10 minutes.

2. In a medium saucepan, combine the vinegar and sugar. Bring to a boil over medium-high heat and cook, stirring constantly, until the sugar has dissolved. Stir in the corn and bell peppers. Return to a boil, reduce to a simmer, cover, and cook until the mixture is slightly syrupy, about 4 minutes. Stir in the scallions, parsley, and ¼ teaspoon of the salt. Remove from the heat and cool slightly.

3. On a plate, combine the cornmeal, flour, bread crumbs, and remaining ½ teaspoon salt. Dredge the chicken in the cornmeal mixture, shaking off the excess. Place the chicken on the prepared baking sheet and bake, turning once, for 25 minutes, or until the chicken is crisp, golden, and cooked through. Place the chicken and corn chowchow on 4 plates and serve.

Suggested accompaniments: Slices of seven-grain bread, and baked apricot halves sprinkled with crumbled gingersnaps to finish.

The sweet-and-sour chowchow, a type of mixed vegetable pickle popular in the South, is a colorful and tangy partner for this satisfying oven-fried chicken. The chowchow can be made up to four days ahead. Simply cover and refrigerate until ready to use, and serve at room temperature for the best flavor.

FAT: 7G/17%
CALORIES: 371
SATURATED FAT: 1.6G
CARBOHYDRATE: 46G
PROTEIN: 32G
CHOLESTEROL: 105MG
SODIUM: 631MG

MUSTARD-CRUMB CHICKEN BREASTS

SERVES: 4
WORKING TIME: 15 MINUTES
TOTAL TIME: 35 MINUTES

The spicy coating for this entrée, flavored with the classic poultry seasonings of rosemary and thyme, is also delicious on chicken thighs or legs. And the tart-and-sweet buttermilk and honey sauce is a perfect companion to the crispy, savory chicken.

¼ cup finely chopped shallots or scallions

3 tablespoons plus 1 teaspoon grainy mustard

3 teaspoons fresh lemon juice

½ teaspoon dried rosemary

¼ teaspoon dried thyme

4 bone-in chicken breast halves (about 1½ pounds total), skinned

½ cup dried bread crumbs

2 teaspoons vegetable oil

½ cup low-fat buttermilk

2 tablespoons chopped fresh parsley

¾ teaspoon honey

¼ teaspoon freshly ground black pepper

¼ teaspoon salt

1. Preheat the oven to 400°. Spray a baking sheet with nonstick cooking spray.

2. In a small bowl, combine 3 tablespoons of the shallots, 3 tablespoons of the mustard, 2 teaspoons of the lemon juice, rosemary, and thyme and stir to blend. Spread the mustard mixture over the skinned side of the chicken, then gently press the bread crumbs into the mustard mixture. Place the chicken on the prepared baking sheet, drizzle with the oil, and bake for 25 minutes, or until the chicken is crisp, golden, and cooked through.

3. Meanwhile, in another small bowl, combine the buttermilk, remaining 1 tablespoon shallots, remaining 1 teaspoon mustard, remaining 1 teaspoon lemon juice, and the parsley, honey, pepper, and salt and stir to blend. Place the chicken on 4 plates and serve with the honey-buttermilk sauce.

Suggested accompaniments: Mixed lettuces with cherry tomatoes and a nonfat Italian dressing, followed by blackberries sprinkled with brown sugar.

FAT: 5G/20%
CALORIES: 229
SATURATED FAT: 1G
CARBOHYDRATE: 14G
PROTEIN: 29G
CHOLESTEROL: 66MG
SODIUM: 484MG

Easy Chicken, Red Beans, and Rice

Serves: 4
Working time: 15 minutes
Total time: 50 minutes

This quickly assembled meal-in-one, based on a Southern classic, is jazzed up with a crisp Parmesan-and-bread crumb topping.

2 teaspoons olive oil

3 cloves garlic, minced

1 large onion, diced

1 green bell pepper, diced

⅔ cup long-grain rice

1 tablespoon no-salt-added tomato paste

1⅔ cups reduced-sodium chicken broth, defatted

16-ounce can red kidney beans, rinsed and drained

½ teaspoon dried marjoram

¾ pound skinless, boneless chicken thighs, cut into 2-inch pieces

1 ounce Canadian bacon, diced

2 tablespoons chopped fresh parsley

2 tablespoons grated Parmesan cheese

2 tablespoons dried bread crumbs

1. Preheat the oven to 350°. In a shallow medium casserole, heat the oil until hot but not smoking over medium-high heat. Add the garlic, onion, and bell pepper and cook, stirring frequently, until the vegetables are tender, about 5 minutes.

2. Add the rice, stirring to coat, and cook for 1 minute. Stir in the tomato paste. Add the broth, kidney beans, and marjoram and cook for 5 minutes longer. Stir in the chicken, bacon, and parsley. Cover, place the casserole in the oven, and bake for 30 minutes, or until the chicken is cooked through and the rice is tender.

3. Preheat the broiler. Sprinkle the Parmesan and bread crumbs over the chicken mixture. Broil the casserole 4 inches from the heat for 2 minutes, or until the topping is crisp and well browned. Spoon the chicken mixture onto 4 plates and serve.

Suggested accompaniments: Tossed salad with an oregano vinaigrette, and dark roast coffee flavored with cinnamon.

FAT: 8G/19%
CALORIES: 388
SATURATED FAT: 1.9G
CARBOHYDRATE: 47G
PROTEIN: 30G
CHOLESTEROL: 76MG
SODIUM: 664MG

SAUTÉS & STIR-FRIES

4

CHICKEN STIR-FRY WITH BROCCOLI, GARLIC, AND BASIL

SERVES: 4
WORKING TIME: 20 MINUTES
TOTAL TIME: 20 MINUTES

Tomato-vegetable juice adds a rich undertone to this intriguing dish—be sure to keep some on hand since it's a great flavor shortcut. As with all stir-fries, cooking is very quick so it's important to have all the ingredients cut and measured beforehand. Also, remember to cut meats and vegetables into small, uniform pieces to ensure even cooking.

2 teaspoons vegetable oil

1 pound skinless, boneless chicken breasts, cut into 2-inch chunks

3 cloves garlic, minced

¼ cup finely chopped scallions

1 tablespoon minced fresh ginger

3 cups broccoli florets

1 cup peeled, thinly sliced broccoli stems

1 cucumber, halved lengthwise and thinly sliced

1 cup cherry tomatoes

5.5-ounce can reduced-sodium tomato-vegetable juice

¾ teaspoon salt

3 tablespoons chopped fresh basil

1. In a large nonstick skillet, heat the oil until hot but not smoking over medium heat. Add the chicken and cook, stirring frequently, until the chicken is no longer pink, about 2 minutes.

2. Add the garlic, scallions, and ginger and cook, stirring constantly, until fragrant, about 30 seconds. Add the broccoli florets and stems, the cucumber, tomatoes, tomato-vegetable juice, and salt. Cook, stirring frequently, until the chicken is cooked through and the broccoli is crisp-tender, about 5 minutes longer.

3. Stir in the basil. Spoon the chicken and vegetables onto 4 plates and serve.

Suggested accompaniments: Steamed white rice, followed by fresh cherries marinated in red wine.

FAT: 4G/18%
CALORIES: 201
SATURATED FAT: .7G
CARBOHYDRATE: 11G
PROTEIN: 30G
CHOLESTEROL: 66MG
SODIUM: 545MG

SWEET AND SOUR CHICKEN

This dish illustrates the yin and yang of sweet and sour flavoring: The tang of vinegar and tomatoes is balanced with a touch of sugar.

⅔ cup long-grain rice

½ teaspoon salt

1 teaspoon olive oil

2 medium onions, chopped

¼ cup cider vinegar

3 cloves garlic, minced

2½ tablespoons sugar

½ teaspoon ground ginger

1 cup reduced-sodium chicken broth, defatted

1 pound skinless, boneless chicken thighs, cut into 1-inch chunks

¾ pound plum tomatoes (about 3), coarsely chopped

1 carrot, thinly sliced

1 green bell pepper, diced

1 red bell pepper, diced

2 cups broccoli florets

1 teaspoon cornstarch

1. In a medium saucepan, combine the rice, 1⅓ cups of water, and ¼ teaspoon of the salt. Bring to a boil over high heat, reduce to a simmer, cover, and cook until the rice is tender, about 17 minutes.

2. Meanwhile, in a large nonstick skillet, heat the oil until hot but not smoking over low heat. Add the onions and cook, stirring frequently, until the onions begin to soften, about 5 minutes. Stir in the vinegar, garlic, sugar, ginger, and remaining ¼ teaspoon salt and cook until the onions begin to caramelize, about 3 minutes.

3. Add the broth. Bring to a boil over medium-high heat and cook until the liquid is slightly reduced, about 3 minutes. Stir in the chicken, tomatoes, carrot, and bell peppers. Return to a boil, reduce to a simmer, cover, and cook for 5 minutes. Add the broccoli, cover, and cook until the chicken is cooked through and the vegetables are tender, about 5 minutes longer.

4. With a slotted spoon, transfer the chicken and vegetables to 4 plates. Return the sauce to a boil over medium-high heat. In a cup, combine the cornstarch and 1 tablespoon of water, stir to blend, and stir into the sauce. Cook, stirring constantly, until the sauce is slightly thickened, about 1 minute. Pour the sauce over the chicken and vegetables, spoon the rice onto the plates, and serve.

Suggested accompaniment: For dessert, honeydew melon wedges drizzled with a warmed mixture of honey and chopped crystallized ginger.

FAT: 7G/16%
CALORIES: 382
SATURATED FAT: 1.4G
CARBOHYDRATE: 52G
PROTEIN: 29G
CHOLESTEROL: 94MG
SODIUM: 564MG

Fajita-Style Fettuccine

SERVES: 4
WORKING TIME: 25 MINUTES
TOTAL TIME: 25 MINUTES

8 ounces fettuccine

¾ pound skinless, boneless chicken breasts, cut into ¼-inch-wide strips

3 cloves garlic, minced

1 red bell pepper, slivered

1 medium red onion, slivered

⅓ cup fresh lemon juice

¼ cup chopped fresh cilantro or parsley

2 teaspoons cornstarch

1 teaspoon dried oregano

1 teaspoon dried basil

½ teaspoon ground cumin

½ teaspoon freshly ground black pepper

¼ teaspoon salt

1 tablespoon olive oil

⅓ cup reduced-sodium chicken broth, defatted

1. In a large pot of boiling water, cook the pasta until just tender. Drain.

2. Meanwhile, in a medium bowl, combine the chicken, garlic, bell pepper, onion, lemon juice, 2 tablespoons of the cilantro, the cornstarch, oregano, basil, cumin, black pepper, and salt and toss gently to coat thoroughly.

3. In a large nonstick skillet, heat the oil until hot but not smoking over medium-high heat. Add the chicken mixture and cook, stirring frequently, until the chicken is cooked through and the vegetables are tender, about 5 minutes.

4. Add the broth and cook, stirring constantly, until the mixture just comes to a simmer, about 1 minute longer. Remove from the heat. Stir in the remaining 2 tablespoons cilantro. Place the pasta on 4 plates, spoon the chicken and vegetables on top, and serve.

Suggested accompaniments: Hearts of romaine lettuce with a nonfat blue cheese dressing. For dessert, lemon ice sprinkled with toasted coconut.

FAT: 7G/17%
CALORIES: 381
SATURATED FAT: 1.2G
CARBOHYDRATE: 50G
PROTEIN: 29G
CHOLESTEROL: 103MG
SODIUM: 262MG

For a new twist on the original Texas fajita, we've substituted chicken for skirt steak, and pasta for tortillas.

CHICKEN, CORN, AND ZUCCHINI SAUTÉ

SERVES: 4
WORKING TIME: 15 MINUTES
TOTAL TIME: 20 MINUTES

2 teaspoons olive oil

1 ounce Canadian bacon, diced

1 zucchini, cut into thin rounds

½ pound mushrooms, thinly sliced

1 pound skinless, boneless chicken breasts, cut into large chunks

1 tablespoon flour

½ cup apple cider or natural apple juice

½ teaspoon salt

1 cup frozen corn kernels

2 tablespoons chopped fresh parsley (optional)

1. In a large nonstick skillet, heat the oil until hot but not smoking over medium heat. Add the bacon and cook until lightly crisped, about 2 minutes. Stir in the zucchini and mushrooms, cover, and cook until the vegetables begin to soften, about 5 minutes.

2. Stir in the chicken and flour and cook, uncovered, stirring frequently, until the chicken is lightly browned, about 2 minutes. Add the cider and salt. Bring to a boil over medium-high heat, reduce to a simmer, cover, and cook until the chicken is cooked through, about 4 minutes.

3. Stir in the corn and cook, uncovered, until the corn is just heated through, about 2 minutes longer. Spoon the chicken and vegetables onto 4 plates, sprinkle with the parsley, and serve.

Suggested accompaniments: Boiled red potato halves tossed with cracked black pepper, followed by peach halves baked with maple syrup.

FAT: 5G/19%
CALORIES: 231
SATURATED FAT: .9G
CARBOHYDRATE: 17G
PROTEIN: 31G
CHOLESTEROL: 69MG
SODIUM: 453MG

Chunky with vegetables and accented with apple cider, this recipe exemplifies simple home cooking. Using just a touch of olive oil mixed with a small amount of smoky Canadian bacon enhances the flavor without overloading on fat. To store mushrooms, refrigerate them, unwashed, in a loosely closed brown paper bag for up to one week.

East-West Chicken Stir-Fry

SERVES: 4
WORKING TIME: 20 MINUTES
TOTAL TIME: 20 MINUTES

For this stir-fry, the pepperiness of watercress, a typical Western ingredient, blends delightfully with the crispness of the water chestnuts, while hot pepper sauce adds just enough heat. Oriental sesame oil, with a deep nutty taste, is used sparingly as a flavor accent.

1 teaspoon Oriental sesame oil
2 red bell peppers, diced
¼ pound mushrooms, cut into quarters
1 pound skinless, boneless chicken breasts, cut into 2-inch chunks
3 cloves garlic, minced
½ cup thinly sliced scallions
2 cups watercress, thick stems trimmed
⅔ cup sliced water chestnuts, rinsed and drained
6 drops hot pepper sauce
½ teaspoon salt

1. In a large nonstick skillet, heat the oil until hot but not smoking over medium heat. Add the bell peppers and mushrooms and cook, stirring frequently, until the vegetables begin to soften, about 2 minutes. Add the chicken and cook, stirring frequently, until the chicken is lightly browned and almost cooked through, about 5 minutes.

2. Stir in the garlic and scallions and cook, stirring frequently, until fragrant, about 1 minute. Add the watercress, water chestnuts, pepper sauce, and salt and stir to coat thoroughly. Cover and cook until the chicken is cooked through and the watercress has wilted, about 2 minutes longer. Spoon the chicken and vegetables onto 4 plates and serve.

Suggested accompaniments: Jasmine tea and thin noodles. For dessert, fresh pineapple wedges sprinkled with brown sugar and broiled.

FAT: 3G/14%
CALORIES: 190
SATURATED FAT: .5G
CARBOHYDRATE: 13G
PROTEIN: 28G
CHOLESTEROL: 66MG
SODIUM: 367MG

CHICKEN AND POTATOES WITH PENNE

SERVES: 4
WORKING TIME: 15 MINUTES
TOTAL TIME: 25 MINUTES

Combining potatoes and pasta is a traditional northern Italian touch that adds both heartiness and texture to this fresh-tasting dish.

6 ounces penne or other tubular pasta

2 teaspoons olive oil

1 ounce Canadian bacon, diced

1 large onion, diced

½ pound all-purpose potatoes, peeled and cut into ½-inch dice

1 pound skinless, boneless chicken breasts, cut into 1-inch chunks

½ pound mushrooms, thinly sliced

2 tablespoons fresh lemon juice

¾ teaspoon salt

½ teaspoon dried rosemary

1 cup chopped plum tomatoes

1. In a large pot of boiling water, cook the pasta until just tender. Drain, return the pasta to the cooking pot, and cover to keep warm.

2. Meanwhile, in a large nonstick skillet, heat the oil until hot but not smoking over medium heat. Add the bacon and onion and cook, stirring frequently, until the onion begins to soften, about 5 minutes. Stir in the potatoes, cover, and cook for 5 minutes.

3. Stir in the chicken, mushrooms, lemon juice, salt, rosemary, and ½ cup of water. Bring to a boil over medium-high heat, reduce to a simmer, cover, and cook until the chicken is cooked through and the potatoes are tender, adding a little more water if the mixture seems dry, about 8 minutes longer.

4. Stir in the tomatoes, pour the sauce over the pasta, and toss to combine. Spoon the chicken-pasta mixture onto 4 plates and serve.

Suggested accompaniment: Thinly sliced navel oranges sprinkled with orange liqueur for dessert.

FAT: 5G/12%
CALORIES: 386
SATURATED FAT: 1G
CARBOHYDRATE: 48G
PROTEIN: 36G
CHOLESTEROL: 69MG
SODIUM: 597MG

FETTUCCINE WITH CHICKEN AND TANGY ONION SAUCE

SERVES: 4
WORKING TIME: 20 MINUTES
TOTAL TIME: 30 MINUTES

6 ounces fettuccine

1 teaspoon vegetable oil

1 pound skinless, boneless chicken thighs, cut into 2-inch chunks

1 large onion, halved and thinly sliced

3 cloves garlic, minced

2 carrots, cut into julienne strips

½ pound mushrooms, cut into quarters

½ teaspoon sugar

½ teaspoon salt

2 tablespoons red wine vinegar

1 scallion, cut into julienne strips

1. In a large pot of boiling water, cook the pasta until just tender. Drain.

2. Meanwhile, in a large nonstick skillet, heat the oil until hot but not smoking over medium heat. Add the chicken and cook, stirring frequently, until lightly browned, about 3 minutes. With a slotted spoon, transfer the chicken to a plate.

3. Add the onion and garlic to the pan and cook, stirring frequently, until the onion begins to soften, about 3 minutes. Add the carrots, mushrooms, sugar, and salt and cook until the vegetables begin to soften, about 4 minutes. Return the chicken to the pan and cook until the chicken is cooked through, about 4 minutes longer.

4. Stir in the vinegar and scallion. Place the pasta on 4 plates, spoon the chicken and vegetables on top, and serve.

Suggested accompaniments: Mixed greens with a mustard vinaigrette. For dessert, fresh fruit salad topped with raspberries puréed with a little red currant jelly.

FAT: 8G/20%
CALORIES: 360
SATURATED FAT: 1.7G
CARBOHYDRATE: 42G
PROTEIN: 31G
CHOLESTEROL: 135MG
SODIUM: 397MG

In *this distinctive dish, a bit of wine vinegar complements the richness of the chicken and mushrooms.*

*F*or our boldly flavored version of a popular Italian specialty, the tomato sauce has chunks of red bell pepper and zucchini for added flavor and texture. Cooking the vegetables first in orange juice imparts an unexpectedly fresh zing.

CHICKEN SCALLOPINI WITH CHUNKY TOMATO SAUCE

SERVES: 4
WORKING TIME: 20 MINUTES
TOTAL TIME: 25 MINUTES

1 tablespoon flour

½ teaspoon salt

¼ teaspoon freshly ground black pepper

4 chicken cutlets (about 1 pound total; see tip)

3 teaspoons olive oil

2 cloves garlic, minced

1 zucchini, halved lengthwise and cut into 1-inch-thick pieces

1 red bell pepper, cut into 1-inch chunks

⅓ cup orange juice

2 tablespoons chopped fresh basil

14½-ounce can no-salt-added stewed tomatoes

1. On a plate, combine the flour, ¼ teaspoon of the salt, and the black pepper. Dredge the chicken in the flour mixture, shaking off the excess. In a large nonstick skillet, heat 2 teaspoons of the oil until hot but not smoking over medium heat. Add the chicken and cook, turning once, until golden brown, about 3 minutes. Transfer the chicken to a plate.

2. Add the remaining 1 teaspoon oil and the garlic to the pan and cook, stirring constantly, until fragrant, about 30 seconds. Stir in the zucchini, bell pepper, orange juice, and basil and increase the heat to medium-high. Cook until the vegetables begin to brown, stirring occasionally, about 3 minutes.

3. Reduce the heat to medium. Stir in the tomatoes and remaining ¼ teaspoon salt. Return the chicken to the pan and cook until the chicken is cooked through and the vegetables are tender, about 3 minutes longer. Place the chicken on 4 plates, spoon the tomato sauce on top, and serve.

Suggested accompaniments: French bread. Follow with angel food cake topped with mandarin orange sections and drizzled with a little Marsala wine.

FAT: 5G/21%
CALORIES: 213
SATURATED FAT: .9G
CARBOHYDRATE: 14G
PROTEIN: 28G
CHOLESTEROL: 66MG
SODIUM: 368MG

TIP

Buy ready-made cutlets or make your own from skinless, boneless chicken breast halves. Holding a knife parallel to the work surface, cut each breast in half horizontally without cutting through to the opposite side. Open the chicken breast like a book, place between sheets of plastic wrap, and pound to an even ¼-inch thickness.

CHICKEN WITH SPAGHETTI AND SUMMER SQUASH

SERVES: 4
WORKING TIME: 20 MINUTES
TOTAL TIME: 20 MINUTES

6 ounces spaghetti

2 teaspoons olive oil

3 cloves garlic, minced

1 pound skinless, boneless chicken thighs, cut into 1-inch chunks

10 ounces yellow summer squash, halved lengthwise and cut into ½-inch-thick pieces

1 red bell pepper, cut into ½-inch chunks

¾ teaspoon dried sage

1½ cups diced plum tomatoes

1 tablespoon red wine vinegar

½ teaspoon salt

2 tablespoons grated Parmesan cheese

1. In a large pot of boiling water, cook the pasta until just tender. Drain.

2. Meanwhile, in a large nonstick skillet, heat the oil until hot but not smoking over low heat. Add the garlic and cook, stirring frequently, until fragrant, about 30 seconds. Increase the heat to medium, add the chicken, and cook, stirring occasionally, until the chicken is lightly browned, about 3 minutes.

3. Add the squash, bell pepper, and sage and cook, stirring frequently, until the vegetables begin to soften, about 3 minutes. Add the tomatoes, vinegar, and salt and cook until the chicken is cooked through and the vegetables are tender, about 4 minutes longer.

4. Place the pasta on 4 plates and spoon the chicken and vegetables on top. Sprinkle with the Parmesan and serve.

Suggested accompaniment: Belgian endive and sliced tomato salad sprinkled with lemon juice and chopped fresh parsley.

This simple chicken sauce is ready in the amount of time it takes to cook the pasta. And you may substitute freely; zucchini for the yellow squash, balsamic vinegar for the red wine vinegar, and dried oregano or rosemary for the sage. Bow-ties or wagon wheels would be fun alternate pasta shapes to use in this dish.

FAT: 8G/21%
CALORIES: 348
SATURATED FAT: 1.6G
CARBOHYDRATE: 40G
PROTEIN: 29G
CHOLESTEROL: 94MG
SODIUM: 380MG

Fresh
asparagus, the
harbinger of spring, is
played to full
advantage against a
background of pasta
and tender chunks of
chicken, all tossed in a
creamy sauce made
with reduced-fat sour
cream. When shopping
for asparagus, select
medium-green, firm,
straight spears with
smooth, unwrinkled
stems and compact tips.

SERVES: 4
WORKING TIME: 20 MINUTES
TOTAL TIME: 20 MINUTES

6 ounces linguine

2 teaspoons olive oil

1 ounce smoked turkey, finely chopped

1 pound skinless, boneless chicken breasts, cut into 1-inch pieces

½ teaspoon salt

¾ pound asparagus, trimmed, peeled (see tip), and cut diagonally into 1-inch pieces

¾ cup reduced-sodium chicken broth, defatted

3 tablespoons light sour cream

2 tablespoons snipped fresh chives or finely chopped scallion

4 teaspoons coarsely chopped pecans

1. In a large pot of boiling water, cook the pasta until just tender. Drain, return the pasta to the cooking pot, and cover to keep warm.

2. Meanwhile, in a large nonstick skillet, heat the oil until hot but not smoking over medium heat. Add the turkey and cook, stirring frequently, until the turkey begins to brown, about 1 minute. Add the chicken and salt and cook, stirring frequently, until the chicken is lightly browned, about 3 minutes.

3. Stir in the asparagus and cook for 1 minute. Add the broth. Bring to a boil over medium-high heat, reduce to a simmer, and cook until the chicken is cooked through and the asparagus is tender, about 3 minutes longer. Remove from the heat. With a slotted spoon, transfer the chicken mixture to the pasta pot.

4. Stir the sour cream and chives into the sauce, pour over the chicken and pasta mixture, and toss to combine. Spoon the chicken-pasta mixture onto 4 plates, sprinkle with the pecans, and serve.

Suggested accompaniments: Shredded carrot salad with a reduced-fat poppy seed dressing, and small scoops of raspberry and orange sherbet for dessert.

TIP

To prepare for cooking, rinse asparagus well, paying particular attention to the tips. Trim off the woody ends. Unless the asparagus is pencil-thin, the outer layers can be tough, so peeling is recommended. Using a swivel-bladed vegetable peeler, remove the outside layers of the stems until you reach the tender centers.

FAT: 8G/20%
CALORIES: 359
SATURATED FAT: 1.7G
CARBOHYDRATE: 35G
PROTEIN: 36G
CHOLESTEROL: 73MG
SODIUM: 543MG

CURRIED CHICKEN BREASTS WITH COCONUT RICE

SERVES: 4
WORKING TIME: 15 MINUTES
TOTAL TIME: 30 MINUTES

*T*he spicy curry sauce is enriched with a secret ingredient—creamy mashed bananas that add a delightful sweetness.

1 cup long-grain rice

3 tablespoons shredded coconut

¾ teaspoon salt

1 tablespoon flour

¼ teaspoon freshly ground black pepper

4 skinless, boneless chicken breast halves (about 1 pound total)

2 teaspoons vegetable oil

2 teaspoons curry powder

2 bananas, coarsely chopped

1 tablespoon fresh lemon juice

1 tablespoon no-salt-added tomato paste

⅛ teaspoon cayenne pepper

1 cup evaporated skimmed milk

½ cup reduced-sodium chicken broth, defatted

1 scallion, thinly sliced

1. In a medium saucepan, combine the rice, coconut, 2 cups of water, and ¼ teaspoon of the salt. Bring to a boil over high heat, reduce to a simmer, cover, and cook until the rice is tender, about 17 minutes.

2. Meanwhile, on a plate, combine the flour, ¼ teaspoon of the salt, and the black pepper. Dredge the chicken in the flour mixture, shaking off the excess. In a large nonstick skillet, heat the oil until hot but not smoking over medium heat. Add the chicken and cook, turning once, until golden brown, about 5 minutes. With a slotted spoon, transfer the chicken to a plate.

3. Add the curry powder to the pan and cook, stirring constantly, until fragrant, about 30 seconds. Add the bananas, lemon juice, tomato paste, and cayenne pepper, mashing the bananas with the back of a spoon. Stir in the evaporated milk, broth, and remaining ¼ teaspoon salt. Return the chicken to the pan. Bring to a boil over medium-high heat, reduce to a simmer, cover, and cook until the chicken is cooked through, about 8 minutes longer.

4. Spoon the curried chicken and rice onto 4 plates. Sprinkle with the scallion and serve.

Suggested accompaniments: Steamed snow peas and carrots and, for dessert, fresh strawberries with vanilla nonfat yogurt for dipping.

FAT: 7G/14%
CALORIES: 445
SATURATED FAT: 1.8G
CARBOHYDRATE: 59G
PROTEIN: 35G
CHOLESTEROL: 76MG
SODIUM: 645MG

SPANISH-STYLE CHICKEN

SERVES: 4
WORKING TIME: 15 MINUTES
TOTAL TIME: 25 MINUTES

4-ounce jar roasted red peppers or pimientos, rinsed and drained

Two 4-ounce cans mild green chilies, rinsed and drained

2 slices firm white sandwich bread, toasted and coarsely torn

¼ cup reduced-sodium chicken broth, defatted

¼ cup dark raisins

2 tablespoons slivered blanched almonds

½ teaspoon seeded, chopped pickled jalapeño pepper

½ teaspoon salt

1 tablespoon flour

¼ teaspoon freshly ground black pepper

4 skinless, boneless chicken breast halves (about 1 pound total)

2 teaspoons vegetable oil

Four 6-inch flour tortillas

2 tablespoons thinly sliced scallion

1. Remove a red pepper half, cut into thin strips, and set aside. In a food processor or blender, combine the remaining red peppers, the chilies, bread, broth, 2 tablespoons of the raisins, 1 tablespoon of the almonds, the jalapeño pepper, and ¼ teaspoon of the salt and purée until smooth.

2. On a plate, combine the flour, the remaining ¼ teaspoon salt, and the black pepper. Dredge the chicken in the flour mixture, shaking off the excess. In a large nonstick skillet, heat the oil until hot but not smoking over medium heat. Add the chicken and cook, turning once, until golden brown, about 5 minutes. Add the pepper purée, bring to a boil over medium-high heat, reduce to a simmer, and cover. Cook until the chicken is cooked through, about 8 minutes longer.

3. Meanwhile, preheat the oven to 350°. Wrap the tortillas in foil and heat for 5 minutes, or until the tortillas are heated through.

4. With a slotted spoon, transfer the chicken to a cutting board and cut the chicken into diagonal slices. Place the tortillas on 4 plates and spoon the chicken and sauce on top. Sprinkle with the remaining 2 tablespoons raisins, remaining 1 tablespoon almonds, reserved pepper strips, and scallion and serve.

Suggested accompaniment: Green seedless grapes and sliced kiwi and nectarine garnished with a sprig of watercress.

FAT: 8G/23%
CALORIES: 319
SATURATED FAT: 1.2G
CARBOHYDRATE: 30G
PROTEIN: 31G
CHOLESTEROL: 66MG
SODIUM: 663MG

Thickening the sauce with bread is a centuries-old Catalan technique that lends subtle flavor and body without fat.

CHICKEN-FRIED PASTA

SERVES: 4
WORKING TIME: 20 MINUTES
TOTAL TIME: 30 MINUTES

Stir-frying the cooked bow-ties with the chicken and vegetables creates a slightly crisp pasta, which is then accented by a final sprinkle of vinegar and soy sauce in this exquisitely flavorful recipe. Store tightly wrapped fresh, unpeeled ginger in the refrigerator for up to a week or in the freezer for up to two months.

6 ounces bow-tie pasta

2 teaspoons peanut oil

1 pound skinless, boneless chicken thighs, cut into 2-inch chunks

4 cloves garlic, minced

2 teaspoons minced fresh ginger

½ teaspoon salt

2 leeks, cut into 2-inch julienne strips

2 carrots, cut into 2-inch julienne strips

½ cup frozen peas

2 tablespoons rice wine vinegar or cider vinegar

2 teaspoons reduced-sodium soy sauce

1. In a large pot of boiling water, cook the pasta until just tender. Drain, rinse under cold water, and drain again.

2. Meanwhile, in a large nonstick skillet, heat the oil until hot but not smoking over medium heat. Add the chicken and cook, stirring frequently, until lightly browned, about 5 minutes. Stir in the garlic, ginger, and salt and cook, stirring frequently, until fragrant, about 1 minute. Add the leeks and carrots and cook until the chicken is almost cooked through and the vegetables are tender, about 3 minutes.

3. Add the pasta and the peas and cook, stirring frequently, until the chicken is cooked through and the pasta is slightly crisp, about 3 minutes longer. Sprinkle with the vinegar and soy sauce. Spoon the chicken-pasta mixture onto 4 plates and serve.

Suggested accompaniments: Sesame bread sticks, and an orange and cucumber salad drizzled with a chive-flavored buttermilk dressing.

FAT: 8G/19%
CALORIES: 384
SATURATED FAT: 1.6G
CARBOHYDRATE: 48G
PROTEIN: 30G
CHOLESTEROL: 94MG
SODIUM: 520MG

The enticing colors are just the beginning of this stir-fry's appeal, which includes the crunch of water chestnuts and lightly cooked bell peppers and snow peas, sharply underscored with the fresh tastes of ginger and orange. Teriyaki sauce, available in the Oriental foods section of the supermarket, gives the chicken a tasty glaze.

STIR-FRIED CHICKEN WITH PEPPERS AND SNOW PEAS

SERVES: 4
WORKING TIME: 20 MINUTES
TOTAL TIME: 20 MINUTES

2 teaspoons Oriental sesame oil

1 pound skinless, boneless chicken breasts, cut into ½-inch-wide strips

1 large onion, halved and cut into thin strips

1 red bell pepper, cut into ½-inch strips

1 green bell pepper, cut into ½-inch strips

3 cloves garlic, minced

2 strips orange zest, each about 3 inches long

1 tablespoon minced fresh ginger

½ teaspoon salt

½ pound snow peas, trimmed and cut diagonally in half (see tip)

8-ounce can sliced water chestnuts, rinsed and drained

2 teaspoons teriyaki sauce

1. In a large nonstick skillet, heat the oil until hot but not smoking over medium heat. Add the chicken and cook, stirring frequently, for 2 minutes. Add the onion, bell peppers, garlic, orange zest, ginger, and salt and cook, stirring frequently, until the chicken is lightly browned, about 3 minutes.

2. Stir in the snow peas, water chestnuts, teriyaki sauce, and 3 table-spoons of water. Increase the heat to high and cook, stirring frequently, until the chicken is cooked through and the vegetables are crisp-tender, about 3 minutes longer. Spoon the chicken and vegetables onto 4 plates and serve.

Suggested accompaniments: Steamed brown rice, and fresh kumquats.

TIP

To prepare snow peas for cooking, trim the stem end and pull off the string along the straight side. For best results, cook snow peas just until they are crisp-tender and a vibrant green.

FAT: 4G/16%
CALORIES: 231
SATURATED FAT: .7G
CARBOHYDRATE: 19G
PROTEIN: 29G
CHOLESTEROL: 66MG
SODIUM: 472MG

CHICKEN CACCIATORE

SERVES: 4
WORKING TIME: 20 MINUTES
TOTAL TIME: 40 MINUTES

This homey favorite, aromatic with wine and herbs, is even better on the second day. Just reheat gently on the stovetop.

1 tablespoon flour

½ teaspoon salt

¼ teaspoon freshly ground black pepper

4 skinless, boneless chicken breast halves (about 1 pound total)

2 teaspoons olive oil

1 large onion, chopped

3 cloves garlic, minced

6 ounces mushrooms, cut into quarters

2 tablespoons brandy or reduced-sodium chicken broth, defatted

⅓ cup dry white wine

1 cup chopped plum tomatoes

3 tablespoons orange juice

1 tablespoon no-salt-added tomato paste

½ teaspoon grated orange zest

½ teaspoon dried rosemary

⅛ teaspoon red pepper flakes

1. On a plate, combine the flour, ¼ teaspoon of the salt, and the pepper. Dredge the chicken in the flour mixture, shaking off the excess. In a large nonstick skillet, heat the oil until hot but not smoking over medium heat. Add the chicken and cook, turning once, until golden brown, about 5 minutes. With a slotted spoon, transfer the chicken to a plate.

2. Add the onion and garlic to the pan and cook until the onion begins to soften, about 5 minutes. Add the mushrooms and cook, stirring frequently, until the mushrooms begin to soften, about 5 minutes. Add the brandy and cook until the liquid has evaporated, about 3 minutes. Add the wine, increase the heat to high, and cook until the liquid has reduced slightly, about 5 minutes.

3. Stir in the tomatoes, orange juice, tomato paste, orange zest, rosemary, red pepper flakes, and the remaining ¼ teaspoon salt and bring to a boil. Return the chicken to the pan, reduce to a simmer, cover, and cook until the chicken is cooked through, about 8 minutes longer. Spoon the chicken and vegetables onto 4 plates and serve.

Suggested accompaniments: Crusty semolina bread, and pears poached with honey and currants for dessert.

FAT: 4G/15%
CALORIES: 233
SATURATED FAT: .7G
CARBOHYDRATE: 12G
PROTEIN: 29G
CHOLESTEROL: 66MG
SODIUM: 358MG

BROILED & GRILLED

5

CHICKEN DIJONNAISE

SERVES: 4
WORKING TIME: 15 MINUTES
TOTAL TIME: 20 MINUTES

The zesty honey-mustard glaze enhances the delicate taste of this chicken, and the cucumber and sweet red pepper relish provides a refreshingly light accent. If you're using a grill, there's no need to heat up the kitchen on a sultry summer evening—all the cooking is done outside.

3 tablespoons Dijon mustard
2 tablespoons honey
4 teaspoons cider vinegar
½ cup finely diced cucumber
½ cup finely diced red bell pepper
½ cup finely diced tomato
3 tablespoons finely chopped scallion
⅛ teaspoon freshly ground black pepper
4 skinless, boneless chicken breast halves (about 1 pound total)

1. Preheat the broiler or prepare the grill. In a 1-cup measure, combine the mustard, honey, and vinegar and stir to blend. Transfer ¼ cup of the honey-mustard mixture to a medium bowl and set aside the remaining mixture.

2. Add the cucumber, bell pepper, tomato, scallion, and black pepper to the ¼ cup honey-mustard mixture and toss to coat.

3. Brush the chicken with the reserved honey-mustard mixture and broil or grill 4 inches from the heat for about 4 minutes per side, or until the chicken is just cooked through. Place the chicken on 4 plates, spoon the cucumber-bell pepper relish on top, and serve.

Suggested accompaniments: Tossed salad with radicchio, cherry tomatoes, and a red wine vinaigrette. For dessert, apple slices sautéed with cranberries and brown sugar.

FAT: 2G/10%
CALORIES: 186
SATURATED FAT: .4G
CARBOHYDRATE: 14G
PROTEIN: 27G
CHOLESTEROL: 66MG
SODIUM: 417MG

ONION-SMOTHERED CHICKEN

SERVES: 4
WORKING TIME: 20 MINUTES
TOTAL TIME: 35 MINUTES

6 tablespoons red wine vinegar

4 teaspoons sugar

½ teaspoon dried sage

½ teaspoon salt

4 skinless, boneless chicken breast halves (about 1 pound total)

2 teaspoons olive oil

2 large onions, halved and thinly sliced

1 cup reduced-sodium chicken broth, defatted

1 tablespoon flour

1 carrot, cut into thin strips

1 red bell pepper, cut into thin strips

¼ teaspoon freshly ground black pepper

1. In a shallow bowl, combine 3 tablespoons of the vinegar, 2 teaspoons of the sugar, ¼ teaspoon of the sage, and ¼ teaspoon of the salt and stir to blend. Add the chicken, toss to coat, and let stand while you prepare the onions.

2. In a large nonstick skillet, heat the oil until hot but not smoking over medium heat. Add the onions and the remaining 2 teaspoons sugar and cook, stirring occasionally, until the onions begin to brown, about 5 minutes. Add the broth and cook until most of the liquid has evaporated, about 5 minutes. Stir in the flour, carrot, bell pepper, remaining 3 tablespoons vinegar, remaining ¼ teaspoon sage, remaining ¼ teaspoon salt, and the black pepper and cook until the onions are very tender and caramelized, about 10 minutes longer.

3. Meanwhile, preheat the broiler or prepare the grill. Broil or grill the chicken 4 inches from the heat for about 4 minutes per side, or until the chicken is just cooked through. Place the chicken on 4 plates, spoon the onion mixture around the chicken, and serve.

Suggested accompaniments: Garlic mashed potatoes made with low-fat milk. Follow with fresh pear wedges sprinkled with cinnamon.

FAT: 4G/16%
CALORIES: 222
SATURATED FAT: .7G
CARBOHYDRATE: 17G
PROTEIN: 28G
CHOLESTEROL: 66MG
SODIUM: 517MG

Here, broiled chicken breasts are deliciously blanketed with a savory onion and sage mélange enlivened with red wine vinegar. Slow-cooking the onions until they caramelize intensifies their natural sweetness and eliminates any bitterness. The onion mixture can be made a day ahead and refrigerated, and then gently reheated at serving time.

SALSA-MARINATED CHICKEN

SERVES: 4
WORKING TIME: 15 MINUTES
TOTAL TIME: 20 MINUTES

This recipe is a good example of how an already excellent store-bought product can become "homemade" with a few simple touches. Jarred salsa is mixed with tomato paste for a no-cook poultry marinade. Then, by adding corn and bell pepper for texture, and lime juice and cilantro for zing, we've created a full-flavored vegetable salsa to serve on the side.

1½ cups good-quality prepared salsa

2 tablespoons no-salt-added tomato paste

4 skinless, boneless chicken breast halves (about 1 pound total)

1 green bell pepper, cut into thin strips

⅔ cup frozen corn kernels, thawed

3 tablespoons finely chopped scallion

2 tablespoons fresh lime juice

2 tablespoons chopped fresh cilantro or parsley

1. Preheat the broiler or prepare the grill. In a shallow bowl, combine ½ cup of the salsa and the tomato paste and stir to blend. Add the chicken, turn to coat, and let stand while you prepare the vegetable salsa.

2. In a medium bowl, combine the remaining 1 cup salsa, the bell pepper, corn, scallion, lime juice, and cilantro.

3. Broil or grill the chicken 4 inches from the heat for about 4 minutes per side, or until the chicken is just cooked through. Place the chicken on 4 plates, spoon the vegetable salsa on the side, and serve.

Suggested accompaniments: Mixed greens with diced avocado sprinkled with a balsamic vinaigrette. For dessert, reduced-calorie vanilla pudding dusted with unsweetened cocoa powder.

FAT: 2G/10%
CALORIES: 182
SATURATED FAT: .4G
CARBOHYDRATE: 14G
PROTEIN: 27G
CHOLESTEROL: 66MG
SODIUM: 530MG

SERVES: 4
WORKING TIME: 10 MINUTES
TOTAL TIME: 20 MINUTES

Red pepper flakes and chili sauce provide the heat for this relish. For a flavor twist, substitute cantaloupe or mango for the pineapple.

16-ounce can crushed pineapple in juice, drained

1 red bell pepper, diced

1 scallion, finely chopped

¼ cup plus 2 tablespoons chili sauce

¼ cup plus 1 tablespoon thawed frozen pineapple juice concentrate

2 tablespoons honey

2 teaspoons red wine vinegar

¼ teaspoon red pepper flakes

4 skinless, boneless chicken breast halves (about 1 pound total)

1. Preheat the broiler or prepare the grill. If using a broiler, line the broiler pan with foil. In a medium bowl, combine the pineapple, bell pepper, scallion, 2 tablespoons of the chili sauce, 1 tablespoon of the pineapple juice concentrate, 1 tablespoon of the honey, the vinegar, and pepper flakes and stir to blend. Let the pineapple-pepper relish stand while you prepare the chicken.

2. In a small bowl, combine the remaining ¼ cup chili sauce, remaining ¼ cup pineapple juice concentrate, and remaining 1 tablespoon honey and stir to blend. Brush the chicken with half of this chili sauce mixture and broil or grill 4 inches from the heat for 4 minutes. Turn the chicken, brush with the remaining chili sauce mixture, and broil or grill for about 4 minutes longer, or until the chicken is just cooked through.

3. Place the chicken on 4 plates, spoon the pineapple-pepper relish on the side, and serve.

Suggested accompaniments: Warm corn tortillas, a green salad with sliced cucumbers and a garlic vinaigrette, and fresh pineapple wedges.

FAT: 2G/6%
CALORIES: 299
SATURATED FAT: .4G
CARBOHYDRATE: 44G
PROTEIN: 28G
CHOLESTEROL: 66MG
SODIUM: 419MG

Barbecued Chicken with Beans

SERVES: 4
WORKING TIME: 25 MINUTES
TOTAL TIME: 40 MINUTES

1 large onion, finely chopped

2 cloves garlic, minced

14½ ounce-can no-salt-added stewed tomatoes

⅓ cup thawed frozen orange juice concentrate

3 tablespoons cider vinegar

2 tablespoons no-salt-added tomato paste

1 tablespoon molasses

1 teaspoon ground ginger

½ teaspoon salt

½ teaspoon grated orange zest

½ teaspoon dry mustard

½ teaspoon cinnamon

8 chicken drumsticks (about 2 pounds total), skinned

19-ounce can red kidney beans, rinsed and drained

1. Preheat the broiler or prepare the grill. If using a broiler, line the broiler pan with foil. In a medium saucepan, combine the onion, garlic, tomatoes, orange juice concentrate, vinegar, 2 tablespoons of water, tomato paste, molasses, ginger, salt, orange zest, mustard, and cinnamon. Bring to a boil over medium-high heat, breaking up the tomatoes with the back of a spoon, reduce to a simmer, and cook, stirring occasionally, until the barbecue sauce is slightly thickened, about 10 minutes.

2. Transfer 1½ cups of the barbecue sauce to a small bowl and brush the chicken generously with this sauce. Broil or grill 6 inches from the heat for about 15 minutes, turning and basting occasionally with the remaining sauce in the bowl, or until the chicken is just cooked through.

3. Stir the beans into the remaining barbecue sauce and cook until the beans are heated through, about 5 minutes. Place the chicken and the beans on 4 plates and serve.

Suggested accompaniments: Cabbage and carrot slaw with a reduced-fat ranch dressing. For dessert, fresh peach slices sprinkled with raspberry vinegar and topped with a dollop of vanilla nonfat yogurt.

FAT: 6G/14%
CALORIES: 373
SATURATED FAT: 1.3G
CARBOHYDRATE: 41G
PROTEIN: 39G
CHOLESTEROL: 110MG
SODIUM: 594MG

The barbecue sauce lends a sweet-tangy finish to the chicken, and also forms the tasty base for our "baked" beans.

CHICKEN AND VEGETABLE KABOBS

SERVES: 4
WORKING TIME: 20 MINUTES
TOTAL TIME: 30 MINUTES

Designed for a festive lunch or light supper, these kabobs are bursting with the aromatic flavors of oregano, rosemary, allspice, and orange zest. To get a head start, you may mix the basting sauce and assemble the kabobs several hours before cooking and store them separately, covered, in the refrigerator.

¾ teaspoon dried oregano

½ teaspoon dried rosemary

¼ teaspoon freshly ground black pepper

¼ teaspoon ground allspice

½ teaspoon salt

¾ pound skinless, boneless chicken breasts, cut into 2-inch pieces

1 red bell pepper, cut into 2-inch squares

1 green bell pepper, cut into 2-inch squares

1 red onion, cut into 2-inch chunks

8-ounce can no-salt-added tomato sauce

½ teaspoon grated orange zest

¼ teaspoon cinnamon

1. Preheat the broiler or prepare the grill. In a large bowl, combine ½ teaspoon of the oregano, the rosemary, black pepper, allspice, and ¼ teaspoon of the salt. Add the chicken, bell peppers, and onion, toss to coat thoroughly, and let stand while you prepare the basting sauce.

2. In a small bowl, combine the tomato sauce, orange zest, cinnamon, the remaining ¼ teaspoon oregano, and remaining ¼ teaspoon salt and stir to blend.

3. Alternately thread the chicken, bell peppers, and onion on 8 skewers. Brush the kabobs with some of the basting sauce and broil or grill 5 inches from the heat for about 8 minutes, turning once halfway through cooking time and basting occasionally with the remaining sauce, or until the chicken is just cooked through. Place the kabobs on 4 plates and serve.

Suggested accompaniments: Potato salad with chopped celery, red onion, and parsley tossed with a low-fat Italian dressing. Finish with graham crackers sandwiched with strawberry nonfat frozen yogurt.

FAT: 1G/9%
CALORIES: 143
SATURATED FAT: .3G
CARBOHYDRATE: 11G
PROTEIN: 21G
CHOLESTEROL: 49MG
SODIUM: 347MG

SERVES: 4
WORKING TIME: 15 MINUTES
TOTAL TIME: 25 MINUTES

This wonderfully flavorful chicken gets its sweetness from ketchup and brown sugar, spiciness from hot pepper sauce, and subtle tanginess from mild rice vinegar. Since vegetables figure heavily in this dish and noodles form the base, there really is no need for any accompaniment, except a simple offering for dessert.

⅔ cup low-sodium ketchup

2 tablespoons rice wine vinegar or cider vinegar

2 teaspoons firmly packed dark brown sugar

½ teaspoon ground coriander

4 cups ¼-inch-thick shredded green cabbage

2 carrots, shredded

6 drops hot pepper sauce

4 skinless, boneless chicken breast halves (about 1 pound total)

4 ounces capellini noodles

⅓ cup finely chopped scallions

2 tablespoons chopped fresh cilantro or mint

1. Preheat the broiler or prepare the grill. If using a broiler, line the broiler pan with foil. Start heating a large pot of water to boiling for the noodles.

2. In a large bowl, combine the ketchup, vinegar, brown sugar, and coriander and stir to blend. Remove 3 tablespoons of the ketchup mixture and set aside. Add the cabbage, carrots, hot pepper sauce, and 2 tablespoons of water to the remaining ketchup mixture in the bowl and toss to coat thoroughly.

3. Brush the chicken with the 3 tablespoons ketchup mixture and broil or grill 4 inches from the heat for about 4 minutes per side, or until the chicken is just cooked through.

4. Cook the noodles in the boiling water until just tender. Drain well. Place the noodles on 4 plates and spoon the cabbage mixture and the chicken on top. Sprinkle with the scallions and cilantro and serve.

Suggested accompaniment: Hazelnut coffee with almond biscotti or meringue cookies.

FAT: 2G/6%
CALORIES: 301
SATURATED FAT: .5G
CARBOHYDRATE: 38G
PROTEIN: 32G
CHOLESTEROL: 66MG
SODIUM: 405MG

CHICKEN WITH CHILI CORN SAUCE

SERVES: 4
WORKING TIME: 15 MINUTES
TOTAL TIME: 25 MINUTES

2 teaspoons medium-hot chili powder

½ teaspoon salt

¼ teaspoon sugar

4 skinless, boneless chicken breast halves (about 1 pound total)

¾ cup reduced-sodium chicken broth, defatted

1 red bell pepper, diced

1 green bell pepper, diced

¾ cup frozen corn kernels

2 tablespoons finely chopped scallion

2 tablespoons fresh lime juice

2 tablespoons light sour cream

1. Preheat the broiler or prepare the grill. In a cup, combine ½ teaspoon of the chili powder, ¼ teaspoon of the salt, and the sugar. Rub the chicken with the chili mixture and let stand while you prepare the chili corn sauce.

2. In a large nonstick skillet, combine the broth, bell peppers, corn, scallion, lime juice, the remaining 1½ teaspoons chili powder, and remaining ¼ teaspoon salt. Bring to a boil over medium-high heat, reduce to a simmer, and cook until the bell peppers are tender and the sauce is slightly thickened, about 7 minutes. Set aside.

3. Broil or grill the chicken 4 inches from the heat for about 4 minutes per side, or until the chicken is just cooked through.

4. Gently rewarm the corn mixture over low heat. Remove from the heat and stir in the sour cream. Place the chicken on 4 plates, spoon the chili corn sauce on top, and serve.

Suggested accompaniments: Grilled French bread. For dessert, applesauce with currants and a dusting of ground nutmeg.

*J*ust a touch of sour cream nicely cools the slightly spicy corn sauce for these chili-rubbed chicken breasts. For easier last-minute preparation, fix the sauce ahead, without the sour cream, and then gently reheat just before serving. Stir in the sour cream off the heat to prevent curdling.

FAT: 3G/14%
CALORIES: 187
SATURATED FAT: .9G
CARBOHYDRATE: 11G
PROTEIN: 29G
CHOLESTEROL: 68MG
SODIUM: 482MG

BROILED CHICKEN WITH APRICOT-LEMON SAUCE

SERVES: 4
WORKING TIME: 15 MINUTES
TOTAL TIME: 35 MINUTES

This lively sauce borrows its inspiration from Middle Eastern ingredients—the dried apricots sweetly underscore the sharp-flavored lemon, mint, and vinegar. Fresh mint is essential in this dish. Refrigerate mint for up to three days, unwashed, upright with stems in water and the tops loosely covered with a plastic bag.

½ cup dried apricots, coarsely chopped

2 cloves garlic, minced

¼ cup fresh lemon juice

3 tablespoons chopped fresh mint

2 tablespoons sugar

1 tablespoon red wine vinegar

1 teaspoon grated lemon zest

4 skinless, boneless chicken breast halves (about 1 pound total)

¼ teaspoon salt

¼ teaspoon freshly ground black pepper

1. In a medium saucepan, combine the apricots, 1 cup of hot water, the garlic, 3 tablespoons of the lemon juice, the mint, sugar, vinegar, and lemon zest. Bring to a boil over high heat, reduce to a simmer, and cook, partially covered, stirring occasionally, until the sauce is thick and glossy, about 20 minutes.

2. Meanwhile, preheat the broiler or prepare the grill. Brush the chicken with the remaining 1 tablespoon lemon juice and sprinkle with the salt and pepper. Broil or grill the chicken 4 inches from the heat for about 4 minutes per side, or until the chicken is just cooked through.

3. Place the chicken on 4 plates, spoon the apricot-lemon sauce on top, and serve.

Suggested accompaniments: Steamed julienne of zucchini and yellow squash. Follow with vanilla ice milk drizzled with a nonfat chocolate sauce.

FAT: 1G/7%
CALORIES: 195
SATURATED FAT: .4G
CARBOHYDRATE: 18G
PROTEIN: 27G
CHOLESTEROL: 66MG
SODIUM: 211MG

Herbed Chicken Breasts with Lentils

Serves: 4
Working time: 10 minutes
Total time: 20 minutes

Red lentils cook very quickly—find them at health food stores. You may substitute regular lentils, but allow 40 minutes cooking time.

½ teaspoon dried thyme
½ teaspoon dried rosemary
¼ teaspoon salt
4 skinless, boneless chicken breast halves (about 1 pound total)
1 cup red lentils
1 cup reduced-sodium chicken broth, defatted
3 cloves garlic, minced
¼ teaspoon ground allspice
¼ teaspoon cinnamon
¼ teaspoon ground ginger
2 scallions, finely chopped

1. Preheat the broiler or prepare the grill. In a cup, combine the thyme, rosemary, and salt. Rub the chicken with the herb mixture and let stand while you prepare the lentils.

2. In a large saucepan, combine the lentils, broth, garlic, allspice, cinnamon, and ginger. Bring to a boil over medium-high heat, reduce to a simmer, cover, and cook until the lentils are slightly crunchy, about 5 minutes. Stir in the scallions.

3. Broil or grill the chicken 4 inches from the heat for about 4 minutes per side, or until the chicken is just cooked through. Spoon the lentil mixture onto 4 plates, place the chicken on top, and serve.

Suggested accompaniments: Sliced, seeded cucumbers marinated in a plain nonfat yogurt dressing and toasted wedges of pita bread. For dessert, a fresh fruit cup.

Fat: 2g/6%
Calories: 300
Saturated Fat: .4g
Carbohydrate: 29g
Protein: 40g
Cholesterol: 66mg
Sodium: 376mg

SPICY JAMAICAN-STYLE CHICKEN THIGHS

SERVES: 4
WORKING TIME: 20 MINUTES
TOTAL TIME: 30 MINUTES

1 scallion, finely chopped

1 clove garlic, minced

1 tablespoon red wine vinegar

2 teaspoons vegetable oil

½ teaspoon cinnamon

½ teaspoon ground allspice

½ teaspoon ground ginger

¼ teaspoon minced pickled jalapeño pepper

⅛ teaspoon freshly ground black pepper

¼ teaspoon salt

4 bone-in chicken thighs (about 1¼ pounds total), skinned

2 Granny Smith apples, peeled, cored, and coarsely chopped

½ cup apple cider or natural apple juice

¼ cup golden raisins

½ teaspoon vanilla extract

1. Preheat the broiler or prepare the grill. In a small bowl, combine the scallion, garlic, vinegar, oil, cinnamon, allspice, ginger, jalapeño pepper, black pepper, and salt and stir to blend. Rub the chicken with the spice mixture and let stand while you prepare the apple-raisin sauce.

2. In a medium saucepan, combine the apples and cider. Bring to a boil over medium-high heat, reduce to a simmer, cover, and cook until the apples are tender, about 10 minutes. Remove from the heat. Stir in the raisins and vanilla. Cover to keep warm.

3. Broil or grill the chicken 6 inches from the heat for about 15 minutes, turning once halfway through cooking time, or until the chicken is just cooked through. Place the chicken and the apple-raisin sauce on 4 plates and serve.

Suggested accompaniments: Basmati or Texmati rice and red grapes. Follow with sliced bananas brushed with red currant jelly and glazed under the broiler.

FAT: 7G/26%
CALORIES: 228
SATURATED FAT: 1.4G
CARBOHYDRATE: 22G
PROTEIN: 21G
CHOLESTEROL: 86MG
SODIUM: 230MG

A fresh, chunky fruit sauce tames the heat from the pickled jalapeño and black pepper on this chicken.

CHICKEN WITH PLUM TOMATO SALSA

SERVES: 4
WORKING TIME: 15 MINUTES
TOTAL TIME: 20 MINUTES

The flavors of several aromatic herbs and spices shine through: cilantro, cumin, and coriander. Both the salsa and chicken can be made up to eight hours ahead and stored separately in the refrigerator. You could also serve the salsa with broiled or grilled fish such as salmon or tuna, or mix it with low-fat cottage cheese for a zesty snack.

½ teaspoon dried oregano

¼ teaspoon ground cumin

¼ teaspoon ground coriander

½ teaspoon salt

4 skinless, boneless chicken breast halves (about 1 pound total)

2 teaspoons olive oil

¾ pound plum tomatoes (about 3), coarsely chopped

½ cup peeled, seeded, and diced cucumber

3 tablespoons chopped fresh cilantro or parsley

2 tablespoons red wine vinegar

⅛ teaspoon cayenne pepper

1. Preheat the broiler or prepare the grill. In a cup, combine the oregano, cumin, coriander, and ¼ teaspoon of the salt. Rub the chicken with the spice mixture, drizzle with the oil, and let stand while you prepare the plum tomato salsa.

2. In a medium bowl, combine the tomatoes, cucumber, cilantro, vinegar, the remaining ¼ teaspoon salt, and the cayenne pepper.

3. Broil or grill the chicken 4 inches from the heat for about 4 minutes per side, or until the chicken is just cooked through. Place the chicken on 4 plates, spoon the plum tomato salsa on top, and serve.

Suggested accompaniments: Couscous with a sprinkling of toasted pine nuts. For dessert, cubed cantaloupe or honeydew melon tossed with lime juice and dusted with crushed amaretti cookies.

FAT: 4G/21%
CALORIES: 173
SATURATED FAT: .7G
CARBOHYDRATE: 6G
PROTEIN: 27G
CHOLESTEROL: 66MG
SODIUM: 360MG

LEMON CHICKEN KABOBS

SERVES: 4
WORKING TIME: 20 MINUTES
TOTAL TIME: 30 MINUTES

4 skinless, boneless chicken breast halves (about 1 pound total), each cut lengthwise into 4 strips

1 zucchini, cut into ½-inch-thick rounds

1 red bell pepper, cut into 1-inch squares

¼ cup fresh lemon juice

1½ teaspoons sugar

1 teaspoon grated lemon zest

¾ teaspoon dried oregano

½ teaspoon salt

4 small pita breads, each cut into quarters

1⅓ cups reduced-sodium chicken broth, defatted

2 cloves garlic, minced

½ teaspoon ground ginger

2 teaspoons cornstarch

2 tablespoons chopped fresh parsley

1. Preheat the broiler or prepare the grill. In a large bowl, combine the chicken, zucchini, bell pepper, 2 tablespoons of the lemon juice, the sugar, lemon zest, oregano, and ¼ teaspoon of the salt and toss to coat thoroughly.

2. Alternately thread the zucchini, chicken, and bell pepper on 8 skewers. Broil or grill the kabobs 5 inches from the heat for about 8 minutes, turning once halfway through cooking time, or until the chicken is just cooked through. Wrap the pitas in foil, place in the broiler or grill with the chicken, and heat for 5 minutes, or until the pitas are warmed through.

3. Meanwhile, in a medium saucepan, combine the broth, remaining 2 tablespoons lemon juice, the garlic, ginger, and remaining ¼ teaspoon salt. Bring to a boil over high heat and cook for 3 minutes. In a cup, combine the cornstarch and 1 tablespoon of water, stir to blend, and stir into the boiling broth. Cook, stirring constantly, until the sauce is slightly thickened, about 1 minute. Stir in the parsley.

4. Place the chicken kabobs and the pitas on 4 plates and serve with the lemon sauce.

Suggested accompaniment: A dessert of grilled nectarine halves sprinkled with brown sugar and topped with a dollop of light sour cream.

FAT: 3G/8%
CALORIES: 319
SATURATED FAT: .5G
CARBOHYDRATE: 39G
PROTEIN: 33G
CHOLESTEROL: 66MG
SODIUM: 867MG

For this simple meal, let each dinner guest slip the succulent chunks of chicken and vegetables into a pita and drizzle with the garlicky lemon sauce. Zucchini and red bell peppers are two vegetables available in good supply all year round. Choose unblemished vegetables with no soft spots or discoloration. Store in a plastic bag in the refrigerator and use within four days.

This
sophisticated entrée
features sharp, peppery
watercress as the
perfect foil for the
sweet and spicy chicken
breasts. The maple
syrup glaze is also a
delectable partner for
lean pork chops.
If watercress is
unavailable, substitute
shredded Belgian
endive, curly endive,
or romaine lettuce.

MAPLE-BROILED CHICKEN

SERVES: 4
WORKING TIME: 15 MINUTES
TOTAL TIME: 30 MINUTES

2 cloves garlic, minced

½ cup maple syrup

½ cup orange juice

1 teaspoon grated orange zest

½ teaspoon dried thyme

½ teaspoon salt

⅛ teaspoon red pepper flakes

1 teaspoon olive oil

1 red bell pepper, cut into thin strips

2 bunches watercress (about 12 ounces), thick stems trimmed

4 bone-in chicken thighs (about 1¼ pounds total), skinned

2 navel oranges, peeled, pith removed, and thinly sliced (see tip)

1. In a medium saucepan, combine the garlic, maple syrup, orange juice, orange zest, thyme, salt, and pepper flakes. Bring to a boil over medium heat and cook until the maple mixture is reduced by one-half, about 5 minutes. Set aside to cool slightly.

2. Meanwhile, preheat the broiler or prepare the grill. If using a broiler, line the broiler pan with foil. In a medium skillet, heat the oil until hot but not smoking over medium heat. Add the bell pepper and cook, stirring occasionally, until the bell pepper begins to soften, about 5 minutes. Add the watercress, cover, and cook until the watercress is wilted, about 5 minutes longer. Set aside.

3. Brush the chicken with half of the maple mixture and broil or grill 6 inches from the heat for 7 minutes. Turn the chicken, brush with the remaining maple mixture, and broil or grill for about 8 minutes longer, or until the chicken is just cooked through.

4. Spoon the watercress mixture onto 4 plates and place the chicken on top. Place the orange slices on the side and serve.

Suggested accompaniments: Orzo or other small pasta. For dessert, toasted slices of fat-free pound cake drizzled with strawberry purée.

FAT: 6G/18%
CALORIES: 300
SATURATED FAT: 1.2G
CARBOHYDRATE: 41G
PROTEIN: 23G
CHOLESTEROL: 86MG
SODIUM: 402MG

TIP

The bitter white pith of an orange, lemon, or lime lies between the flesh of the fruit and the zest. Use a small, sharp paring knife to cut away the white pith from the flesh of the peeled fruit; discard the pith.

CHICKEN TERIYAKI

SERVES: 4
WORKING TIME: 20 MINUTES
TOTAL TIME: 35 MINUTES

The *honey glaze caramelizes as these kabobs cook, imparting a golden color to the chicken and a deeply rich flavor. If using wooden skewers, be sure to soak them in cold water for ten minutes first to prevent burning. Cherry tomatoes, sold year-round, are especially sweet. Try the yellow variety that are often found at the end of the summer at farmstands.*

1½ tablespoons reduced-sodium soy sauce

1 tablespoon honey

1 teaspoon ground ginger

½ teaspoon Oriental sesame oil

1 clove garlic, peeled and crushed

1 pound skinless, boneless chicken breasts, cut into 2-inch pieces

⅔ cup long-grain rice

¼ teaspoon salt

1 green bell pepper, cut into 1-inch squares

1 pint cherry tomatoes

2 scallions, finely chopped

1. In a shallow bowl, combine the soy sauce, honey, ginger, sesame oil, and garlic and stir to blend. Add the chicken, toss to coat thoroughly, and let stand while you start the rice.

2. In a medium saucepan, combine the rice, 1⅓ cups of water, and the salt. Bring to a boil over high heat, reduce to a simmer, cover, and cook until the rice is tender, about 17 minutes.

3. Meanwhile, preheat the broiler or prepare the grill. Alternately thread the chicken, bell pepper, and tomatoes on 8 skewers. Broil or grill the kabobs 5 inches from the heat, turning once halfway through cooking time, for about 8 minutes, or until the chicken is just cooked through.

4. Stir the scallions into the rice. Spoon the rice mixture onto 4 plates, place the kabobs on top, and serve.

Suggested accompaniments: Green leaf lettuce and red onion salad with an orange vinaigrette. Follow with poached plums topped with bits of candied ginger.

FAT: 2G/6%
CALORIES: 283
SATURATED FAT: .5G
CARBOHYDRATE: 34G
PROTEIN: 30G
CHOLESTEROL: 66MG
SODIUM: 444MG

GLOSSARY

Allspice—A dark, round, dried berry about the size of a peppercorn, called allspice because it tastes like a combination of cloves, cinnamon, and nutmeg. Usually sold in ground form, allspice is often mistakenly thought to be a blend of several spices.

Basil—An herb with a flavor somewhere between clove and licorice. Fresh basil will maintain more fragrance if added at the end of cooking. Dried basil is a good deal milder than fresh, but can still be used to good advantage in soups, stews, sauces, and marinades. To store, refrigerate fresh basil, unwashed, stem ends in a jar of water and tops loosely covered with a plastic bag, for up to 3 days.

Chives—A mild-flavored member of the onion family distinguished by long, green shoots. Because their subtle flavor is lost when heated, add chives to a cooked dish at the last minute. Snip rather than chop chives to avoid crushing.

Chop—To roughly cut an ingredient into small pieces—not as uniform as a dice and not as fine as a mince. Flavor will permeate a dish with still a hint of texture. Anchor the tip of a knife with your hand, keeping fingers away from the sharp edge, and quickly lift and lower the knife handle, slowly swinging the blade across the food.

Chutney—A sweet, spicy condiment ranging from smooth to chunky, generally made of fruit. Chutney is most often used in Indian cooking, especially as an accompaniment to curries.

Cilantro/Coriander—The lacy green leaves of the coriander plant are the herb cilantro. It has a pungent taste, and is often used in Mexican and Oriental cooking. To store, wash the leaves, shaking off water, wrap in paper towels, and refrigerate for up to a week. The seeds of the coriander plant, considered a spice, have a different flavor than the fresh, bordering on citrusy. Coriander seeds are sold whole or as a ground powder.

Cumin—A pungent, peppery-tasting spice essential to many Middle Eastern, Asian, Mexican, and Mediterranean dishes. Available ground or as whole seeds; the seeds are often toasted in a dry skillet to bring out their flavor.

Currants—Tiny raisins made from a small variety of grape. Use interchangeably with raisins, especially in sauces and rice dishes, keeping in mind that currants are smaller and will disperse more flavor and sweetness.

Curry powder—Not one spice but a mix of spices, commonly used in Indian cooking to flavor a dish with sweet heat and add a characteristic yellow-orange color. While curry blends vary (consisting of as many as 20 herbs and spices), they typically include turmeric for its vivid yellow color, ginger, cloves, cumin, coriander, and cayenne pepper. Commercially available Madras curry is hotter than other store-bought types.

Dice—To cut food into small, uniform squares of ⅛ to ¼ inch, adding visual interest and texture to a dish. To dice, cut the ingredient into uniform strips, depending on how small or large you want the dice. Then cut the strips crosswise.

Dill—A name given to both the fresh herb and the small, hard, dried seeds that are used as a spice. Add the light, lemony, fresh dill leaves (also called dillweed) at the end of cooking. Dried dill seeds provide a distinctive sour note and marry well with sour cream- or yogurt-based dishes.

Drizzling with oil—To uniformly disperse a measured amount of oil over food. Holding a spoon with measured oil, shake gently from side to side, drizzling the entire surface.

Dutch ovens—Large saucepots or flameproof casseroles with ear handles and tight-fitting covers; useful both for stovetop and oven cooking. For the recipes in this book, use a Dutch oven with a 4- to 5-quart capacity that has been treated with a nonstick coating.

Ginger—A thin-skinned root used as a pungent seasoning. Fresh ginger is good tossed into a stir-fry or sauté for a peppery, slightly sweet flavor. Tightly wrapped, unpeeled fresh ginger can be refrigerated for 1 week or frozen for up to 2 months. Ground ginger is not a true substitute for fresh, but it will lend a warming flavor to soups, stews, and sauces.

Hoisin sauce—A thick, slightly sweet sauce used in Chinese cooking, made from soybeans, chilies, garlic, and spices. Once opened, it will keep in the refrigerator for several months.

Hot pepper sauce—A highly incendiary sauce made from a variety of hot peppers flavored with vinegar and salt. Use sparingly, drop by drop, to introduce a hot edge to any dish, especially barbecue sauces, rice dishes, and gumbos.

Julienne—Thin, uniform, matchstick-size pieces of an ingredient, usually a vegetable, typically 2 inches long. Cut the food into long, thin slices. Then stack the slices and cut lengthwise into sticks, and then crosswise into the desired length.

Marjoram—A member of the mint family that tastes like mildly sweet oregano. Fresh marjoram should be added at the end of cooking so the flavor doesn't vanish. Dried marjoram, sold in leaf and ground form (the more intense leaf being preferable), stands up to longer cooking.

Mince—To cut an ingredient into very small pieces, finer than a chop, so flavor infuses the dish and the pieces themselves practically disappear when cooked. Mincing is usually done to foods that provide background flavor, such as scallions, garlic, ginger, and onions. The technique of stabilizing the point end and rocking the knife on the work surface is the same as for chopping.

Mint—A large family of herbs used to impart a perfumy, heady flavor and a cool aftertaste to foods, the most common being spearmint. As with other fresh herbs, it is best added at the end of cooking. Since dried mint is fairly intense, a pinch is usually all that is needed in cooking. Store fresh mint the same way as basil.

Nutmeg—The hard, brown seed of the nutmeg tree. This spice lasts almost indefinitely, and you grate it freshly as needed on a special grater or an ordinary box grater to add a sweet, nutty spiciness to both desserts and savory dishes. Ground nutmeg offers about the same flavor but with less pungency.

Okra—A small, tapered green pod with a flavor reminiscent of asparagus. When cooked in liquid, okra acts as a thickener, adding body with no extra fat. It's a favorite in Southern cooking, especially for gumbos. If using fresh, choose plump, firm, bright green pods no more than 3 inches long and store in the refrigerator, unwashed, for up to 2 days.

Olive oil—A monounsaturated fat thought to lower blood cholesterol. Olive oil is available in different grades, based on levels of acidity resulting from the method of refining. The best, most expensive oil with the lowest acidity is cold-pressed extra-virgin, primarily used for flavoring sauces and salad dressings. Virgin and pure olive oils are slightly more acidic with less olive flavor, and are ideal for cooking.

Olives—Small, oval fruits available in dozens of varieties from all parts of the world. Chopped, sliced, or added whole, their presence is recognized by a distinctive earthy flavor. Use sparingly, since olives, whether brine-cured or dry-cured, do contain fat and salt, the latter from processing.

Oregano—A member of the mint family characterized by small, green leaves. Prized for its pleasantly bitter taste, oregano is essential to many Mediterranean-style dishes. The dried version is actually more potent than the fresh.

Orzo—A rice-shape pasta, excellent for soups and stews, and a delicious alternative to rice.

Paprika—A spice ground from a variety of red peppers and used in many traditional Hungarian and Spanish preparations. Paprika colors foods a characteristic brick-red and flavors dishes from sweet to spicy-hot, depending on the pepper potency.

Parmesan—A full-flavored, hard grating cheese, very good for low-fat cooking because a little goes a long way. It is used as a tangy garnish or in sauces, stews, or soups to thicken and season. Buy Parmesan in blocks and grate it as needed for best flavor and freshness.

Parsley—A popular herb available in two varieties. Frilly-sprig curly parsley is quite mild, while the flat-leaf Italian parsley has a stronger "green" flavor. Wrap washed parsley in paper towels, slip into plastic bags, and refrigerate for up to 1 week. Since fresh parsley is so available, there is really no reason to use dried.

Parsnip—A beige-colored winter root vegetable that becomes nutty and almost sweet when cooked. To prepare for cooking, simply peel and cut into slices or chunks to toss into soups and stews. Refrigerate parsnips, unwashed, in a perforated plastic bag for up to 1 week, or longer if they remain firm.

Pearl onions—Mild-flavored onions, about ½ inch in diameter, used in stews, soups, braises, and saucy sautés for their crunchy texture and picture-perfect size. A bag of the frozen version is an excellent substitute for the fresh.

Rosemary—An aromatic herb with needle-shaped leaves. Fresh rosemary has a strong, piny flavor that is best used sparingly. The dried version, leaf or ground, retains many of the flavor characteristics of the fresh.

Sage—An intensely fragrant herb with grayish-green leaves. Sage will infuse a dish with a pleasant, musty mint taste. In its dried form, sage is sold as whole leaves, ground, and in a fluffy "rubbed" version. The dried leaves are especially suited for marinades, while sprigs of fresh make a simple garnish.

Saucepans—Deep all-purpose pans (with long handles), ranging in size from 2 cups to 6 quarts; saucepans should be the size specified in the recipe or cooking times may be affected. For the recipes in this book, a small saucepan has a 1-quart capacity; medium 2 to 2½ quarts; large 3 to 4 quarts. As a general rule, saucepans should be as heavy as possible for even cooking.

Scallions—Immature onions (also called green onions) with a mild and slightly sweet flavor. Both the white bulb and the green tops can be used in cooking; the green tops, cut into sections, sliced, or chopped, make an attractive garnish. To prepare, trim off the base of the bulb or root end and any blemished ends of the green tops. Remove the outermost, thin skin around the bulb. Cut the white portion from the green tops and use separately, or use together in the same dish.

Sesame oil, Oriental—A dark, polyunsaturated oil pressed from toasted sesame seeds, used as a flavor enhancer in many Asian and Indian dishes. A lighter colored counterpart, which

is cold-pressed from untoasted sesame seeds, imparts a much milder background note. Store either version in the refrigerator for up to 6 months.

Shallots—A member of the onion family, looking rather like large cloves of garlic. Shallots are used to infuse savory dishes with a mild, delicate onion flavor. Refrigerate for no more than 1 week to maintain maximum flavor.

Shred—To cut an ingredient into narrow, uneven strips to add texture to a dish, almost creating a thickening effect. Cooked meat can be shredded by cutting it apart along the grain with a knife, or by pulling it apart by hand.

Skillets (nonstick)—Broad, 2-inch-deep frying pans coated with a nonstick surface. These treated skillets minimize or eliminate the need for added fat while browning meats or vegetables. Protect the pan's surface by using only nylon, rubber, or wooden utensils, and by cleaning with a soft sponge. For the recipes here, you will need a small (6 inches), a medium (8 inches), and 1 or 2 large (10 to 12 inches) nonstick skillets.

Soy sauce—A condiment made from fermented soybeans, wheat, and salt used to add a salty, slightly sweet flavor to food. Soy sauce is especially at home in stir-fries and other Oriental-style preparations. Keep in mind that reduced-sodium sauces add the same flavor but much less sodium.

Tarragon—A potent, sweet herb with a licorice- or anise-like flavor, with a special affinity for chicken. Tarragon should be used judiciously since the effect can be overwhelming. Dried tarragon loses its potency quickly. Check for flavor intensity every few months—crush a little between your fingers and sniff for the strong aroma. As with most herbs, you may substitute 1 teaspoon dried for every tablespoon fresh.

Thyme—A lemony-tasting member of the mint family frequently paired with bay leaves in Mediterranean-style dishes and rice-based preparations. The dried herb, both ground and leaf, is an excellent substitute for the fresh.

Truss—To tie a whole chicken before roasting, so it keeps a compact shape during cooking. For a simple truss, tie the ends of the drumsticks together with kitchen string. For a sturdier truss, also tie a piece of string around the skin of the neck, leaving 2 long ends of string. Lift the ends of the wings up and over the back of the bird, pass the string over the wings, and tie together so the wings hug the top of the bird.

Turmeric—A root used in Indian cooking as well as in preparing curry powder. When dried and ground, this spice is valued more for its ability to color dishes a vivid yellow-orange than for its bitter, pungent flavor. It's a sensible coloring substitute for the more extravagantly expensive saffron.

Turnip—A winter root vegetable commonly used in soups and stews for its bitter-sweet flavor and slight crunch. Available all year round, turnips have a peak season from October to February. When shopping, look for small turnips with unblemished skins, which have the mildest flavor.

Watercress—A slightly peppery-tasting aquatic herb used to add zip to sautés and stir-fries when chopped and tossed in at the end of cooking. Watercress is also an assertive base for green salads. To prepare, rinse under cold water and blot dry with paper towels. Remove the tough stem ends or, for a more delicate flavor, use just the leaves.

INDEX

Arroz con Pollo, 70
Asian Chicken Roll-Ups, 87

Baked chicken
See also Casseroles
Asian Chicken Roll-Ups, 87
Baked Chicken in Parchment, 86
Baked Chicken with Citrus Sauce, 97
Buffalo Chicken Strips, 84
Chicken and Sweet Potatoes with Rosemary, 89
Chicken Burgers with Sweet Potato Chips, 81
Chicken Parmesan with Herbed Tomatoes, 83
Chicken Pot Pie, 77
Chili-"Fried" Chicken with Rice Pilaf, 73
Crispy Chicken with Corn Chowchow, 98
Glazed Honey-Mustard Chicken, 82
Herbed Chicken with Orzo and Spinach, 74
Mustard-Crumb Chicken Breasts, 101
Oven-Barbecued Chicken Breasts, 94
Spinach-and-Cheese-Stuffed Chicken, 93
Barbecued chicken
See also Grilled chicken
Barbecued Chicken with Beans, 135
Chicken and Vegetable Kabobs, 137
Chicken Breasts with Pineapple-Pepper Relish, 134
Hot and Tangy Barbecued Chicken with Noodles, 139
Oven-Barbecued Chicken Breasts, 94
Boning [chicken] thighs, 9
Braised chicken
Arroz con Pollo, 70
Chicken and Apples Normandy, 48

Chicken Fricassee with Leeks and Peas, 69
Chicken in Green Sauce, 57
Chicken in Red Wine Sauce, 51
Chicken Picante, 66
Chicken with Tomatoes and Chick-Peas, 61
Chicken with Winter Squash and Artichokes, 53
Oven-Braised Rosemary Chicken with Vegetables, 50
Port-Braised Chicken with Carrots and Parsnips, 65
Spiced Chicken Couscous, 47
Broiled/grilled chicken
Barbecued Chicken with Beans, 135
Broiled Chicken and Orange Salad, 27
Broiled Chicken with Apricot-Lemon Sauce, 143
Chicken and Vegetable Kabobs, 137
Chicken Breasts with Pineapple-Pepper Relish, 134
Chicken Dijonnaise, 129
Chicken Teriyaki, 153
Chicken with Chili Corn Sauce, 140
Chicken with Plum Tomato Salsa, 147
Herbed Chicken Breasts with Lentils, 144
Hot and Tangy Barbecued Chicken with Noodles, 139
Lemon Chicken Kabobs, 148
Maple-Broiled Chicken, 151
Onion-Smothered Chicken, 130
Salsa-Marinated Chicken, 133
Spicy Jamaican-Style Chicken Thighs, 145
Broth, Homemade Chicken, 9
Browning, about, 10
Buffalo Chicken Strips, 84
Burgers, Chicken, with Sweet Potato Chips, 81

Buying chicken, 8

Cacciatore, Chicken, 126
Caramelizing, about, 10
Caribbean Chicken Salad, 13
Casseroles
See also Braised chicken; Stews
Chicken Pot Pie, 77
Chicken, Vegetables, and Corn Bread Casserole, 95
Easy Chicken, Red Beans, and Rice, 102
Chicken, about
See also Chicken cooking techniques
Buying chicken, 8
Handling chicken, 8
Chicken breasts
See also Chicken cutlets
Baked Chicken in Parchment, 86
Baked Chicken with Citrus Sauce, 97
Broiled Chicken with Apricot-Lemon Sauce, 143
Chicken and Apples Normandy, 48
Chicken and Sweet Potatoes with Rosemary, 89
Chicken Breasts with Pineapple-Pepper Relish, 134
Chicken Cacciatore, 126
Chicken Dijonnaise, 129
Chicken in Green Sauce, 57
Chicken Parmesan with Herbed Tomatoes, 83
Chicken Picante, 66
Chicken with Chili Corn Sauce, 140
Chicken with Plum Tomato Salsa, 147
Chicken with Winter Squash and Artichokes, 53

Chili-"Fried" Chicken with Rice Pilaf, 73
Curried Chicken Breasts with Coconut Rice, 120
Glazed Honey-Mustard Chicken, 82
Herbed Chicken Breasts with Lentils, 144
Herbed Chicken with Orzo and Spinach, 74
Hot and Tangy Barbecued Chicken with Noodles, 139
Mustard-Crumb Chicken Breasts, 101
Onion-Smothered Chicken, 130
Oven-Barbecued Chicken Breasts, 94
Oven-Braised Rosemary Chicken with Vegetables, 50
Salsa-Marinated Chicken, 133
Spinach-and-Cheese-Stuffed Chicken, 93
Chicken cooking techniques
Boning thighs, 9
Skinning legs and breasts, 8
Splitting whole legs, 8
Stuffing under skin, 9
Chicken cutlets
Chicken Scallopini with Chunky Tomato Sauce, 115
Chicken drumsticks
Barbecued Chicken with Beans, 135
Port-Braised Chicken with Carrots and Parsnips, 65
Savory Chicken, Carrot, and Potato Stew, 45
Chicken legs
See also Drumsticks; Thighs
Crispy Chicken with Corn Chowchow, 98
Chicken salads
Broiled Chicken and Orange Salad, 27
Caribbean Chicken Salad, 13

Chicken and Potato Salad, 31
Chicken and White Bean Salad, 24
Chicken Cobb Salad, 42
Chicken Tabbouleh Salad, 37
Chinese Chicken Salad with Peanuts, 33
Mediterranean Chicken Salad, 23
New Deli Chicken Salad, 41
Taco Salad with Tomato-Avocado Salsa, 19
Chicken thighs
    Chicken Fricassee with Leeks and Peas, 69
    Chicken in Red Wine Sauce, 51
    Chicken with Tomatoes and Chick-Peas, 61
    Maple-Broiled Chicken, 151
    Spicy Jamaican-Style Chicken Thighs, 145
Chili, Chunky Chicken and Corn, 55
Chili-"Fried" Chicken with Rice Pilaf, 73
Chinese Chicken Salad with Peanuts, 33
Chowder, Hearty Chicken and Corn, 21
Cobb Salad, Chicken, 42
Cooking techniques. *See Techniques, cooking*
Couscous, Spiced Chicken, 47
Curried Chicken Breasts with Coconut Rice,
    120

Dredging, about, 10
Dumplings, Parslied Chicken and, 63

East-West Chicken Stir-Fry, 111
Easy Chicken, Red Beans, and Rice, 102

Fajita-Style Fettuccine, 107
Fat, Skimming, 10
Fricassee, Chicken, with Leeks and Peas, 69

Goulash, Chicken, with Egg Noodles, 58
Grilled chicken. *See Broiled/grilled chicken*
Gumbo, Louisiana-Style Chicken, 15

Homemade Chicken Broth, 9

Jamaican-Style Chicken Thighs, Spicy, 145
Jambalaya, Chicken, 56

Kabobs
    Chicken and Vegetable Kabobs, 137
    Chicken Teriyaki, 153
    Lemon Chicken Kabobs, 148

Louisiana-Style Chicken Gumbo, 15

Maple-Broiled Chicken, 151
Mediterranean Chicken Salad, 23
Mom's Chicken Noodle Soup, 39

New Deli Chicken Salad, 41

Onion-Smothered Chicken, 130
Oriental Chicken Soup, 25
Oven-Barbecued Chicken Breasts, 94
Oven-Braised Rosemary Chicken with
    Vegetables, 50

Port-Braised Chicken with Carrots and
                    Parsnips, 65
Pot Pie, Chicken, 77

Reducing, about, 10

Roast chicken
    Lemon Chicken with Roast Potatoes and
        Garlic, 91
    Roast Chicken with Pecan-Rice Dressing, 79
Roll-Ups, Asian Chicken, 87

Salads. *See Chicken salads*
Salsa-Marinated Chicken, 133
Sautéed/Stir-fried chicken
    Chicken and Potatoes with Penne, 112
    Chicken Cacciatore, 126
    Chicken Stir-Fry with Broccoli, Garlic, and
        Basil, 105
    Chicken with Spaghetti and Summer Squash,
        116
    Chicken, Corn, and Zucchini Sauté, 108
    Chicken-Fried Pasta, 123
    Curried Chicken Breasts with Coconut Rice,
        120
    East-West Chicken Stir-Fry, 111
    Fajita-Style Fettuccine, 107
    Fettuccine with Chicken and Tangy Onion
        Sauce, 113
    Spanish-Style Chicken, 121
    Stir-Fried Chicken and Asparagus with
        Linguine, 119
    Stir-Fried Chicken with Peppers and Snow
        Peas, 125
    Sweet and Sour Chicken, 106
Scallopini, Chicken, with Chunky Tomato
    Sauce, 115
Skimming fat, 10
Skinning [chicken] legs and breasts, 8

Soups
    Chicken and Winter Vegetable Soup, 34
    Creamy Chicken Soup with Vegetables, 28
    Hearty Chicken and Corn Chowder, 21
    Lemon-Dill Chicken and Rice Soup, 16
    Louisiana-Style Chicken Gumbo, 15
    Mom's Chicken Noodle Soup, 39
    Oriental Chicken Soup, 25
Spanish-Style Chicken, 121
Splitting whole [chicken] legs, 8
Stews
    Chicken Goulash with Egg Noodles, 58
    Chicken Jambalaya, 56
    Chunky Chicken and Corn Chili, 55
    Parslied Chicken and Dumplings, 63
    Savory Chicken, Carrot, and Potato Stew, 45
Stir-Fries. *See Sautéed/Stir-fried chicken*
Stuffing [chicken] under skin, 9
Sweet and Sour Chicken, 106

Tabbouleh Salad, Chicken, 37
Taco Salad with Tomato-Avocado Salsa, 19
Techniques, cooking
    See also Chicken cooking techniques
    Browning, about, 10
    Caramelizing, about, 10
    Dredging, about, 10
    Reducing, about, 10
    Skimming fat, 10
    Zesting, about, 7
Teriyaki, Chicken, 153

Zesting, about, 7

Time-Life Books is a division of Time Life Inc.

PRESIDENT and CEO: John M. Fahey, Jr.
EDITOR-IN-CHIEF: John L. Papanek

TIME-LIFE BOOKS

MANAGING EDITOR: Roberta Conlan

Director of Design: Michael Hentges
Director of Editorial Operations: Ellen Robling
Director of Photography and Research: John Conrad Weiser
Senior Editors: Russell B. Adams, Jr., Dale M. Brown, Janet Cave,
    Lee Hassig, Robert Somerville, Henry Woodhead
Director of Technology: Eileen Bradley
Library: Louise D. Forstall

PRESIDENT: John D. Hall

Vice President, Director of Marketing: Nancy K. Jones
Vice President, Director of New Product Development: Neil Kagan
Associate Director, New Product Development: Quentin S. McAndrew
Marketing Director, New Product Development: Robin B. Shuster
Director of Finance: Christopher Hearing
Vice President, Book Production: Marjann Caldwell
Production Manager: Marlene Zack
Consulting Editor: Catherine Boland Hackett
Special Contributors: Sally Collins, Barbara Sause

Design for Great Taste-Low Fat by David Fridberg of
Miles Fridberg Molinaroli, Inc.

 REBUS, INC.
PUBLISHER: Rodney M. Friedman
EDITORIAL DIRECTOR: Charles L. Mee

Editorial Staff for *Chicken*
Director, Recipe Development and Photography: Grace Young
Editorial Director: Kate Slate
Recipe Developer: Sandra Rose Gluck
Managing Editor: Janet Charatan
Production Editor: Susan Paige
Writer: David J. Ricketts
Nutritionists: Hill Nutrition Associates

Art Director: Sara Bowman
Associate Art Director: Jennifer Chung
Photographers: Lisa Koenig, Vincent Lee
Photographers' Assistants: Eugene DeLucie, Rainer Fehringer
Food Stylists: A.J. Battifarano, Andrea B. Swenson, Karen J.M. Tack
Assistant Food Stylists: Marie Baker-Lee, Amy Lord
Prop Stylist: Sara Abalan

TIME-LIFE is a trademark of Time Warner Inc. U.S.A.

Library of Congress Cataloging-in-Publication Data

Chicken.
    p.   cm. -- (Great taste, low fat)
Includes index.
ISBN 0-7835-4550-9 (alk. paper)
1. Cookery (Chicken) 2. Low-fat diet--Recipes. 3. Quick and easy
cookery. I. Time-Life Books. II. Series
TX750.5.C45C4473   1995
641.6'65--dc20
                                 95-17784
                                    CIP

Other Publications
THE TIME-LIFE COMPLETE GARDENER
JOURNEY THROUGH THE MIND AND BODY
WEIGHT WATCHERS® SMART CHOICE RECIPE COLLECTION
TRUE CRIME
THE AMERICAN INDIANS
THE ART OF WOODWORKING
LOST CIVILIZATIONS
ECHOES OF GLORY
THE NEW FACE OF WAR
HOW THINGS WORK
WINGS OF WAR
CREATIVE EVERYDAY COOKING
COLLECTOR'S LIBRARY OF THE UNKNOWN
CLASSICS OF WORLD WAR II
TIME-LIFE LIBRARY OF CURIOUS AND UNUSUAL FACTS
AMERICAN COUNTRY
VOYAGE THROUGH THE UNIVERSE
THE THIRD REICH
MYSTERIES OF THE UNKNOWN
TIME FRAME
FIX IT YOURSELF
FITNESS, HEALTH & NUTRITION
SUCCESSFUL PARENTING
HEALTHY HOME COOKING
UNDERSTANDING COMPUTERS
LIBRARY OF NATIONS
THE ENCHANTED WORLD
THE KODAK LIBRARY OF CREATIVE PHOTOGRAPHY
GREAT MEALS IN MINUTES
THE CIVIL WAR
PLANET EARTH
COLLECTOR'S LIBRARY OF THE CIVIL WAR
THE EPIC OF FLIGHT
THE GOOD COOK
WORLD WAR II
THE OLD WEST

*For information on and a full description of any of the Time-Life Books series
listed above, please call 1-800-621-7026 or write:*
Reader Information
Time-Life Customer Service
P.O. Box C-32068
Richmond, Virginia 23261-2068

METRIC CONVERSION CHARTS

VOLUME EQUIVALENTS
(fluid ounces/milliliters and liters)

US	Metric
1 tsp	5 ml
1 tbsp (½ fl oz)	15 ml
¼ cup (2 fl oz)	60 ml
⅓ cup	80 ml
½ cup (4 fl oz)	120 ml
⅔ cup	160 ml
¾ cup (6 fl oz)	180 ml
1 cup (8 fl oz)	240 ml
1 qt (32 fl oz)	950 ml
1 qt + 3 tbsps	1 L
1 gal (128 fl oz)	4 L

Conversion formula
Fluid ounces X 30 = milliliters
1000 milliliters = 1 liter

WEIGHT EQUIVALENTS
(ounces and pounds/grams and kilograms)

US	Metric
¼ oz	7 g
½ oz	15 g
¾ oz	20 g
1 oz	30 g
8 oz (½ lb)	225 g
12 oz (¾ lb)	340 g
16 oz (1 lb)	455 g
35 oz (2.2 lbs)	1 kg

Conversion formula
Ounces X 28.35 = grams
1000 grams = 1 kilogram

LINEAR EQUIVALENTS
(inches and feet/centimeters and meters)

US	Metric
¼ in	.75 cm
½ in	1.5 cm
¾ in	1 cm
1 in	2.5 cm
6 in	15 cm
12 in (1 ft)	30 cm
39 in	1 m

Conversion formula
Inches X 2.54 = centimeters
100 centimeters = 1 meter

TEMPERATURE EQUIVALENTS
(Fahrenheit/Celsius)

US	Metric
0° (freezer temperature)	-18°
32° (water freezes)	0°
98.6°	37°
180° (water simmers*)	82°
212° (water boils*)	100°
250° (low oven)	120°
350° (moderate oven)	175°
425° (hot oven)	220°
500° (very hot oven)	260°
*at sea level	

Conversion formula
Degrees Fahrenheit minus
32 ÷ 1.8 = degrees Celsius